S0-ACC-434

The Common Core Guidebook™:
Informational Text Lessons

6-8

Rozlyn Linder

Guided Practice, Suggested Book Lists, and Reproducible Organizers

The Common Core Guidebook™, 6-8:
INFORMATIONAL TEXT LESSONS

Guided Practice, Suggested Book Lists, and Reproducible Organizers

Rozlyn Linder, Ph.D.

The Literacy Initiative

Atlanta

The Common Core Guidebook™, 6-8: Informational Text Lessons
www.CommonCoreGuidebook.com

THE COMMON CORE GUIDEBOOK is a trademark of The Literacy Initiative, LLC.
541 Tenth Street Suite 258, Atlanta, Georgia 30318

Permission is granted for teachers to photocopy the reproducible pages from this book for classroom use. No other part of this publication may be reproduced in whole or in part by any electronic or mechanical means, including information storage and retrieval systems, or otherwise, without permission in writing from the publisher, except by a reviewer, who may quote brief passages in a review.

Cover and Interior Design: Buzz Branding, LLC.

Library of Congress Cataloging-in-Publication Data
CIP data is on file with the Library of Congress.
ISBN: 978-0-9889505-0-4

Copyright @2013 by Rozlyn Linder
All rights reserved. Published by The Literacy Initiative, LLC.

Printed in the U. S. A.

For Brooke and Sydney

CONTENTS

CONTENTS

ORGANIZATION OF THIS BOOK

This book is organized to provide guidance for explicit skill instruction for each element of the Common Core informational text reading standards. Each element relies on strong teacher background knowledge, introduction of skills through accessible, real-world understandings, think-aloud modeling by the teacher, guided-practice opportunities, and finally individual application of the strategies with independent texts. *The Common Core Guidebook* is not a replacement for your curriculum. It is, however, a framework of strategies and resources to support the understanding of the informational text reading standards.

THEORETICAL FRAMEWORK

This book relies on the *gradual release* model of reading instruction (Pearson & Gallagher, 1983). Derived from a model used for comprehension strategies, this approach offers a reliable instructional routine that scaffolds and provides support for skill development. The responsibility for the use of a strategy transfers from the teacher to collaborative, and eventually to independent application.

Each skill should be explicitly introduced by the teacher, with most of the initial accountability lying with the teacher. Think-aloud modeling is where the teacher begins to show students the process that he or she uses to make sense of text and implement the specific skill. The practice opportunities are developed so that teachers can offer joint responsibility through collaborative and guided practice and eventually release the full responsibility to the students. Each section of this book, guided by the literacy research on the gradual release model, is a critical component to delivering your instruction of the Common Core informational text standards. There is one chapter for each standard.

Each chapter is organized into four components:

- ► **Understand the Standard**
- ► **Introduce the Standard**
- ► **Think-Aloud Modeling with the Standard**
- ► **Practice the Standard**

UNDERSTAND THE STANDARD

This is about you, as a teacher, making sure that you have expert knowledge of the standard. What key skills do students need? What essential knowledge is critical? You are positioning yourself as an expert. This is the section of the book that gives you the guidance and background to confirm your understanding of each element of the standard. Research indicates that alignment between instruction and standards is often weak (Polikoff, 2012; Spillane, 2004). Your understanding of the standards is a key variable to effectively impacting student achievement.

INTRODUCE THE STANDARD

This section is where you take the core elements of the standard and connect them with your kids. Independent of any text, this is your chance to make connections with the skill they will be learning and their real lives. You want to think outside of the box and find a way to explain the core of the concept in relationship to what matters to them or what they already understand and can make sense of. Your goal is to make the learning concrete and relevant. Vygotsky (1978) asserts that all learning goes from concrete to abstract. This section is where you are attempting to reach an access point from which all kids can build a concrete foundation, regardless of reading levels or ability. This is the anticipatory element that frames the learning from a nonthreatening angle. You are simply making sense of the skill in a way that is concrete and clear. You will note that this section is the most social and relies on high levels of interaction between you and your students.

THINK-ALOUD MODELING WITH THE STANDARD

Think-aloud modeling is the core of the instruction. Now that you have made a connection between the skill and more accessible knowledge, you are going to think-aloud to model how you would use the skills embedded in each standard to make meaning of text. There are two bodies of research from which this section draws. First is the data on the effectiveness of modeling for students; the second is the empirical evidence on the value of the think-aloud protocol.

Modeling for students is an explicit component of scaffolding instruction. This is essential across any content area. You will find that modeling is particularly important for struggling readers who have yet to connect the skills with the process of application.

Research Based

If teachers provide modeling, with a clear purpose, learning occurs.

(Hinchman & Sheridan- Thomas, 2008)

Think-aloud modeling is where the teacher actually lets students see the process that we, as adults, use to make sense of text and implement the specific skills. While no one can capture all of the inner workings of the mind, the think-aloud offers students a snapshot of the mind's eye. The think-aloud helps demonstrate the cognitive process (Davey, 1983). This explicit moment creates a map of the interpretive road upon which a reader travels to make meaning. Effective teachers talk about their thinking as they do it.

An extension to this strategy is to invite students to think-aloud with you. This places value on how readers can verbalize and think about text. You want to guide students through your thought process and invite them to consider their own. Modeling your thinking and asking students to do the same is a process that helps students to enhance their own self-monitoring abilities (Baumann, Jones, & Seifert-

Kessel, 1993). Students become partners with you as you walk them through your own navigational methods for using the strategies embedded in the standard to negotiate textual meaning. This process leads to better discussions about text and a more thorough understanding of text (Oster, 2001). As a teacher, I want students to repeatedly hear how I navigate text and apply strategies.

PRACTICE THE STANDARD

The *Practice the Standard* section has ready-to-use graphic organizers that can extend learning through formative assessment, guided practice, and independent practice.

FORMATIVE ASSESSMENT

Formative assessments are ongoing evaluations and observations of student understanding (Fisher & Frey, 2007). These assessments differ from assessments *of* learning and are really assessments *for* learning. These are practice opportunities for students to apply the skills and strategies that they have developed to independent or guided tasks. The graphic organizers included in this book can be used as formative assessments for student learning. Remember that formative assessments do not need to be graded and are used to inform you of where your students are. This information should help you make decisions about where to go next with your instructional plan. *Do you need to reteach? How differentiated should your lessons be? Should you scaffold and release responsibility to students at a slower or faster pace?* These questions are answered by frequent and consistent formative assessment opportunities. These organizers are lucid opportunities to do just that and support the learning process.

When you use the organizers as formative assessments, be careful to consider what comes next. Assessments should drive your future instruction and inform students of their progress. Middle school students should also be able to self-assess and join you in the process of examining where they are and where they need to go. Assessing and looking at learning can and should be a collaborative process. This means that you need to have conversations, ask students to consider their own metacognition, and share their thoughts about what they are doing and how they make sense of the text. You want to help students not just look for their understandings, but to catch misunderstandings along the way. Teachers need to aggressively check for understanding and make sure that students have a chance to 'get it' before it is too late (Wiggins, 2005).

GUIDED PRACTICE

As you observe and collect data on your students, you will notice that many need additional support. This is when you use the organizers to guide their practice and reteach. This can be organized in several different ways: small group, one-on-one, or in pairs. I like to group students who have demonstrated similar understandings (or misunderstandings) together and work with them through teacher-driven guided practice. Talking with readers about what they are doing or where they are getting confused in order to offer strategies and redirection is crucial. Guided practice provides an up-close opportunity to scaffold instruction and provide substantive feedback (Almasi & Fullerton, 2012). Each standard in this book has an organizer completed through guided practice based on exemplars listed in the Common Core appendices (National Governors Association Center & Council of Chief State School Officers, 2010) or news articles. The same text was selected for consistent models within each standard. Walking students through those examples and helping them to apply the strategies to other informational text is an appropriate way to scaffold and offer support for students.

INDEPENDENT PRACTICE

As students begin to build their knowledge base, the key with the Common Core standards is to ensure that students continue to refine and practice the skills that they have learned. There are multiple ways to do this. The organizers can be assigned as homework, serve as classroom activities, or become standing practice opportunities in literacy centers or stations. Students can select organizers that they find demonstrate their own learning or meet the purpose of a larger assignment. Many schools rely on reading incentive programs where students take multiple-choice tests on the computer or through their media centers. I encourage teachers to have students use an organizer to practice or reinforce a skill along with the basic recall test that many of these programs use. Pair the skill-based practice with the assessment; this encourages students to use a much more critical eye and extend their thinking in ways that a knowledge-level quiz simply cannot. The variations of methods for using the organizers to meet students' needs are endless.

Throughout *The Common Core Guidebook*, you will notice different signs and symbols. These signposts are there to point out or reinforce important information.

This symbol indicates some Common Core terminology that students will hear and read often in the standards.

This icon indicates a link to the writing standards.

These are key ideas to reinforce that are central to your instruction. Don't forget these tips and pointers!

Here you'll discover what the empirical evidence or research says about specific practices or strategies.

Watch out! When you see this symbol, you will get some advice about what to avoid or be careful of in your classroom.

Here are some ways to extend students' thinking or differentiate instruction.

THE NEW SHINY PRETTY

Every so many years, there seems to be some shift in education. The pattern is inevitably uniform each time.

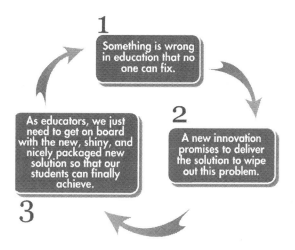

This is the phenomenon that I have dubbed: *The New Shiny Pretty*. In almost two decades as a public school educator, I have seen new instructional reform models, new standards, and shifts in assessments numerous times. Each time, a new focus is lauded as the great savior of education. In fact, I have gotten pretty good at reading through the rhetoric and sorting out exactly what is usually just a new name for an old idea. I am used to shuffling what I already do around and renaming it whatever *The New Shiny Pretty* has determined is the new title for what we are already doing.

My natural inclination when I first heard about the new Common Core standards was to assume that it was time for the latest and greatest *New Shiny*

Pretty and that this was it. I resisted doing much more than printing out the standards and reading over them a few times. As an English teacher, this seemed like what I already did. Honestly, how much can reading change? It is always about reading, writing, and language. *The New Shiny Pretty* might label the parts differently, but the parts are still the same. As I began my usual process of sorting out where the new and old lined up, I kept coming to roadblocks. Some of the skills that had persevered through other reforms seemed to be missing. Some of the new skills used language that I had only seen in my college classes. These Common Core standards were not what I thought they would be. The standards required a different mindset, a new way of looking at literacy for educators, and a new set of strategies. Something was amiss with this *New Shiny Pretty*. It didn't just seem to shine things up and repackage them. This was, dare I say it, different. My theory about nothing being new in education was tossed on its backside.

CHECKLIST TEACHING

Whether it is because of increased accountability or the rise in high-stakes testing, what we, as teachers, have gotten very good at is the Checklist Method of teaching. We simply check off behaviors that are associated with literacy. For example, if successful readers should be able to recognize cause/effect relationships, we teach our students how to recognize a cause/effect relationship and test to see if they can do it. When we finish that, we move on to other indicators of literacy. At the end of our units, we expect students to *apply* these skills. Often the application is in the form of a multiple choice test where students use skills like cause/effect, sequencing, or drawing conclusions to pick the correct answer from a set of four choices about a text. This is how we have taught literacy for a while. Students in third grade do it this way. Students in eighth grade do it this way. High school seniors do it this way. Those who can select the correct response have mastered skills. Unfortunately these students go off to college and are asked to analyze text and write about it. This is when the hammer drops; they cannot do it.

Research Based

Teaching skills and standards has to become recursive. Understanding that skills can be applied to multiple texts and opportunities to practice this application are key. Developing critical thinking skills and an awareness of what to do when they encounter informational text is crucial.

"Let students read frequently. Holding students back because they have not mastered all of the requisite skills is ineffective. Give students the skills, but let them practice and hone those skills with books. Students need multiple opportunities to engage with text to grow as readers."

(Anderson, Wilson, and Fielding, 1995)

JUST PLAY TENNIS

Understanding how the Common Core standards differ from what teachers have primarily done in the past requires a new way of looking at literacy. The Common Core standards do not expect students to only demonstrate mastery of skills in isolation. The Common Core informational text standards demand that students continuously perform skills in concert, with an eye on recursive practice and mastery.

A great analogy to understand this shift in thinking is to compare Common Core literacy to playing a sport. An individual sport like golf or tennis is a perfect comparison. The students are playing a game of their own; they are "doing literacy." Just as Serena Williams or Gabby Douglas must use multiple skills, techniques, and strategies in their sports, so do our students.

Compare the training that Serena Williams has to the average ALTA tennis player. If they learned to play tennis under the Checklist Method of teaching skills and testing them, both Serena and the ALTA player would have been identified as masters of the sport. Do they both know how to serve? Check. Do they both know how to volley? Check. Do they both know the rules of the game? Check. Do they both understand how to hit backhands? Check.

Key Point

Common Core literacy is the opposite of Checklist teaching.

Under the Checklist Method, both are adequate tennis players. In reality, Serena and the average ALTA player could hardly even play a game together. It would be a shutout. I imagine that Serena's serves would probably never even be returned. So—what went wrong? They both learned the same skills. We checked them off. We are sure that they mastered the skills. What exactly happened? This is the same thing that happens in classrooms. Teachers are teaching skills, checking for understanding, and moving on to their other (typically state-mandated) requirements for instruction. The teaching is not the problem. The problem is that the Checklist Method does not produce tennis players. It produces people who can demonstrate skills related to tennis, but cannot use them in concert or independently. This is the same in the class. The Checklist Method does not result in students who can "do literacy." It produces people who know something about literacy and literacy-related behaviors. Despite this knowledge they can't "do literacy."

Often students are held back from progressing to more complex, higher-level skills until they master previous skills. With the Common Core standards students will have explicit skill instruction, but continue to perfect those skills as they are introduced to others. Consider the tennis analogy again here. You don't move to the backhand once your forehand is perfect. If that was the case, you would never get to the backhand. You aren't forbidden to serve if you cannot volley. Imagine if that was how you learned to play tennis. When would you get to play in a game? We have

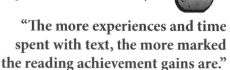

Research Based

"The more experiences and time spent with text, the more marked the reading achievement gains are."

(National Institute of Child Health and Human Development, 2000)

to get students out on the court and let them play the game, observe them so we can offer feedback, and coach them on their weaknesses. Students cannot wait to "do literacy" until they have all the skills perfected. They have to practice "doing literacy" on concrete, on courts with tattered nets, on indoor courts, in bad weather, on hot days, and when it is a bit chilly. If they just work on skills and never use them in concert independently, when they have to play the game — they won't be able to.

DECONSTRUCTING TEXT

"Doing literacy" is something that schools have rarely done well consistently. In fact, I am not sure if we have ever truly taught students to "do literacy." This is one of the major shifts that Common Core suggests. What Common Core proposes is that teachers abandon the Checklist Method of instruction and teach students to do ONE thing. That is not an error; you did not read the text wrong. You teach students one thing under Common Core. You don't teach reading, writing, comprehension, or grammar. Common Core literacy teachers are only tasked with teaching one thing:

We teach students to independently deconstruct text and communicate about it.

Key Point

As students move to the college level, this deconstruction evolves into what traditionally has been described as rhetorical analysis. The language and the descriptors may change, but the core is the same—text deconstruction. Text means images, digital media, and print. How do students take apart text? This is what we want to explicitly teach them how to do so that they can apply it to varying types of text. Many people struggle with this because they want to center their instruction on a particular author or genre. Those things are fine, but they are not the purpose, they are the tools. The focus is not on *The Hobbit*, John Steinbeck, or Sandra Cisneros. The focus is on taking apart text. Students learn to take apart text and use those same skills when they encounter new and unfamiliar text.

The more students spend time actually reading and "doing literacy", the more they develop fluency, linguistic competence, and confidence *(Caldwell & Gaine, 2000)*. **The more you put them on the court, the better they are at the sport.**

THE MIDDLE SCHOOL STANDARDS

Research Based

"...we need to consider the multiple and overlapping forms of literacy, including digital, visual, spoken, and printed forms that require the reader to critically analyze, deconstruct, and reconstruct meaning across a variety of texts for various purposes."

(Mandel Morrow, Gambrell, & Duke, p. 48)

Theoretically, moving away from being a Checklist Teacher to teaching text deconstruction is the most critical step for Common Core teachers. To make this a reality, teachers need a strong understanding of what they have to actually teach in the classroom. When I first began to get ready to bring the Common Core standards into my classroom, I read everything I could get my hands on. The more I read, the more convoluted the standards seemed. Well, luckily for all of us, Common Core is actually a nice tidy list that makes sense—you just need the right lens to rip away all of the "extra" stuff and focus on the standards. That is precisely what *The Common Core Guidebook* does. When you teach students about informational text, you are only teaching NINE standards. Consider these to be your **RI** (Reading Informational Text) **Standards.**

RI 1.	**TEXTUAL EVIDENCE**
RI 2.	**CENTRAL IDEAS**
RI 3.	**CONNECTIONS & RELATIONSHIPS**
RI 4.	**WORD PLAY**
RI 5.	**TEXT STRUCTURE**
RI 6.	**AUTHOR'S POINT OF VIEW**
RI 7.	**BEYOND TEXT**
RI 8.	**EVALUATING EVIDENCE**
RI 9.	**DIFFERENT VIEWPOINTS**

You may notice that standard ten is missing. That is intentional. Standard ten reads as:

6th: By the end of the year, read and comprehend literary nonfiction in the grades 6–8 text complexity band proficiently, with scaffolding as needed at the high end of the range.

7th: By the end of the year, read and comprehend literary nonfiction in the grades 6–8 text complexity band proficiently, with scaffolding as needed at the high end of the range.

8th: By the end of the year, read and comprehend literary nonfiction at the high end of the grades 6–8 text complexity band independently and proficiently.

Key Point

(RI) Standard ten is a teacher standard, not a student standard.

This is a standard for the teacher, not the students. Your students are not trying to prove to you that they are reading increasingly complex text throughout the year. That is your job. You are in charge of suggesting text and introducing them. Don't make that a student standard; teach the other standards and provide varying text throughout the ten months that you have your students.

Textual Evidence

"A wise man proportions his beliefs to the evidence."
-David Hume, philosopher

READING INFORMATIONAL TEXT STANDARD 1:
TEXTUAL EVIDENCE

Sixth	Seventh	Eighth
Cite textual evidence to support analysis of what the text says explicitly as well as inferences drawn from the text.	Cite several pieces of textual evidence to support analysis of what the text says explicitly as well as inferences drawn from the text.	Cite the textual evidence that most strongly supports an analysis of what the text says explicitly as well as inferences drawn from the text.

GRADE LEVEL DIFFERENCES

Students in all grade levels need to be able to cite textual evidence, but with increasing rigor. Sixth graders just need to cite it. Seventh graders need to cite multiple pieces of evidence. Eighth graders are expected to cite multiple pieces and make some judgment calls about the stronger pieces of evidence.

Textual evidence is the core of argument and analysis. Textual evidence is support lifted directly from text to support inferences, claims, and assertions. Think critically about this. The Textual Evidence standard is really about students supporting how they know something. There is a lot of buzz about text-dependent questions and requiring students to refer to the text, but isn't that what good readers do already? This is the opposite of giving a memory test, camouflaged as a reading test, to assess comprehension. You know the type of assessment where kids can't use their book to complete a reading test? They have to prove that they have memorized the facts and details, then answer knowledge questions about what they read earlier. The Textual Evidence standard relies on the direct opposite theoretical perspective. This standard demands that readers engage with the text and share what specific aspects of the text influence their thinking. Instead of asking what the central idea is, teachers now want to rely on the addition of four words: *How do you know?* How do you know what the central idea of the text is? What proof do you have? This is where the Textual Evidence standard pushes students to.

When you plan instruction, this is the first standard that you need to explicitly teach. All of the other informational text standards rely on students being able to actively make inferences and find evidence in a text to support these inferences. There are two different types of things that anyone can say after reading a text. One is that they noticed something that was **explicit**. These are those things that are stated directly in the text. For example: *Andrew Carnegie gave large amounts of money to charity.* If the text spells that information out for the reader, it is explicit; the textual evidence is the actual statement. The other types of things that we notice are **implicit**. We make meaning based on clues from the text. The Common Core standards refer to these as **inferences**. Students need direct textual evidence to support inferences. *Andrew Carnegie was a hard worker.* This could be an example of an inference that a student might make after reading about Carnegie's life. The text may never state explicitly that he was a hard worker, but specific lines of text might support this inference. What this standard has done is demand that students break that into chunks. *What do you infer? How do you know?*

When thinking about how to teach this standard with informational text, you want to target the inferences. Many materials or lesson ideas call for students to explain the **explicit** meaning of a text and point to textual evidence. That requires a very low depth of knowledge. If the text states it right there, in plain English, the students don't have to think about textual evidence at all. To meet the rigor of this standard, students have to make an **inference**, determine what textual evidence supports it, and begin to make judgments about the strength of that support.

1 **Lead a discussion about how students make inferences in their own lives.** *"Have you ever believed something was true based on a feeling you had? Maybe no one directly said it was true, but you could just feel it? Has this ever happened to anyone before? When you draw conclusions based on clues, these are called inferences. An inference is something that you know based on evidence you have seen or read, not because it was spelled out for you."*

2 **Encourage students to share examples from their own life.** Volunteer a life experience of your own (real or imagined) that demonstrates this as well. Every time someone shares, avoid making judgments about the content of what they are saying, but focus on using the vocabulary words of this standard. Rephrase their stories back to them. *"So you could **infer** that your mom was upset even though she didn't come right out and say it **explicitly?"***

3 **Model a "wordless" scene and ask students to make inferences.** *"Let's try that out today. I want everyone to be completely silent and watch me. I am going to walk around and I want you to think about what types of decisions you can make about me based on clues that you notice. When you have made a decision about me, write it down. We are going to call those decisions inferences. So write down what you infer about me based on clues (evidence) that you see. Everyone ready?"*

Key Point

"Inferring is the bedrock of comprehension, not only in reading. We infer in many realms. Our life clicks along more smoothly if we can read the world as well as text."

(Harvey & Goudvis, 2000, p. 105)

4 **Spend two or three minutes demonstrating a strong dislike or like for something in the room.** I typically select one gender that I demonstrate a preference for. I circulate around the room and visibly glare unhappily at either the boys or the girls. I avoid contact with their desks while offering exaggerated smiles and visual clues to indicate which group I prefer. Ham it up and have some fun here. If it doesn't feel silly, you aren't doing it right! This activity should be lighthearted and fun.

5 **Have students share their inferences. Next, ask students how they know that their inferences are correct.** *"How do you know? What evidence do you have that I prefer boys (girls) over girls (boys)?"* The students will think that this is a silly question. You may hear that it was obvious because of how you acted. Point out that you did not come out and say anything at all. *"How do you know? What evidence do you have?"*

6 **List the responses, referring to them as evidence.** Explain that from now on students will make inferences about what they read and provide evidence to support their inferences.

16

1 **Select a short informational text excerpt.** This could come from the suggested list at the end of this chapter or your own collection.

2 **Project the text or give a photocopy to each student.** *"I am going to show you very clearly how I make inferences and back them up with evidence."*

3 **Read the text aloud with students.** This is also a dual opportunity to think-aloud and annotate to demonstrate how you actually read a text closely. I know it sounds silly to say your thoughts out loud, but do it! I even suggest using a "cold" text so that students get your natural thought process and see what a reader really should do.

4 **After reading the text, think-aloud about the text.** *"So what can I say about this text? What inference can I make? Is there anything that I think this author is trying to make me think? What is it? What does this author believe?"* Answer these questions out loud or jot them in the margin, demonstrating your thought process.

5 **Make a few different claims about the text and narrow it down to one.** *"I've got it!"* Write INFERENCE followed by your assertion. *"Now that I have my inference, how can I prove that I am right? What evidence is in the text? What is my textual evidence?"*

6 **Underline, highlight, circle, or copy sentences; there is no magic bullet. Just isolate all of the parts that support your inference.** As you do this, remember to think out loud. Deliberately go to some parts that are NOT textual evidence and let students hear your conversation with the text as you choose not to select those parts as evidence.

Research Based

Teaching students to make inferences requires repeated modeling.

(Zweirs, 2010)

7 Take all of your information and record it on a large anchor chart that can be displayed in the room for later reference. There are great chart and organizer ideas at the end of this chapter. Invite students to share their questions, concerns, and thoughts.

The Organizers

Once you have explicitly introduced and modeled how to apply the strategies of the standard, now is the time to shift gears and provide students with multiple opportunities to practice the skill with their own reading in pairs, groups, and independently.

Students always need models, so each organizer in the Textual Evidence section has been completed based on *A Night to Remember* by Walter Lord. This text is suggested within the Common Core appendices as an appropriate informational text under the social studies strand. This particular text is used for each example under the Textual Evidence standard for consistency and to offer the same book as a point of comparison for teachers.

1 Read (or reread) the first four pages of *A Night to Remember* with students. If you don't have a copy for each student, project the text so that all students can read it. It is important for the Textual Evidence standard that students see the structure and words. Reading aloud alone will be ineffective here. Model how to complete the organizer using the samples that I have modeled next to each organizer or complete your own sample from the blank copy found in each section.

2 Once you model by explicitly completing the organizer yourself, your students will see the connection between the informational text and the organizer. You can provide blank copies of the organizer and allow students to select their own informational text, assign one from your class anthology, or select a title from the suggested book list within this chapter.

3 Students can complete the organizer when they read any informational text. This can be done as an assignment and can be repeated as many times as you want with any informational text that you choose. The sky is the limit! This allows for multiple opportunities to tailor the text to the student and maintain fidelity to the standard.

4 Once students have demonstrated mastery of the skill, don't stop using it. You want them to keep practicing. In the introduction of the book, I discussed the pitfalls of being a Checklist Teacher. Students need to keep perfecting their skill sets.

5 Reuse the same organizer, make it into an anchor chart, or post exemplars for students to reference later. You can add the organizer to a Textual Evidence center, pair it with your school's reading incentive program to focus on Common Core skills with all reading activities, or use it daily as evidence of reading.

STAIR STEPS

Low on copies? This organizer is an easy choice for students to recreate independently on notebook paper.

I like to project this organizer on the interactive whiteboard and encourage students to think along with me, adding to the staircase as we go.

Stair Steps **Text:** A Night to Remember

The night time bakers were not seen as important.

Frederick was a simple, nonglamorous man (unlike the passengers.

"The honor of baking fancy pastry was reserved for the day shift.
Pg. 4

Warnings about the iceberg were not taken very seriously.

... that was all another world to Frederick Fleet.
Pg. 1-2

"Iceberg right ahead," replied Fleet.
"Thank You," acknowledged the voice with detached courtesy.
Pg. 2

Consider enlarging this chart. After you model it, you can display it in the class as a long-term reference chart.

Teach students to use ellipses and grammatical shorthand on the organizers. You want to focus on content, not surface structures.

©2013 The Common Core Guidebook. Intended for classroom use only. May not be reproduced or distributed without permission.

Stair Steps

Text:

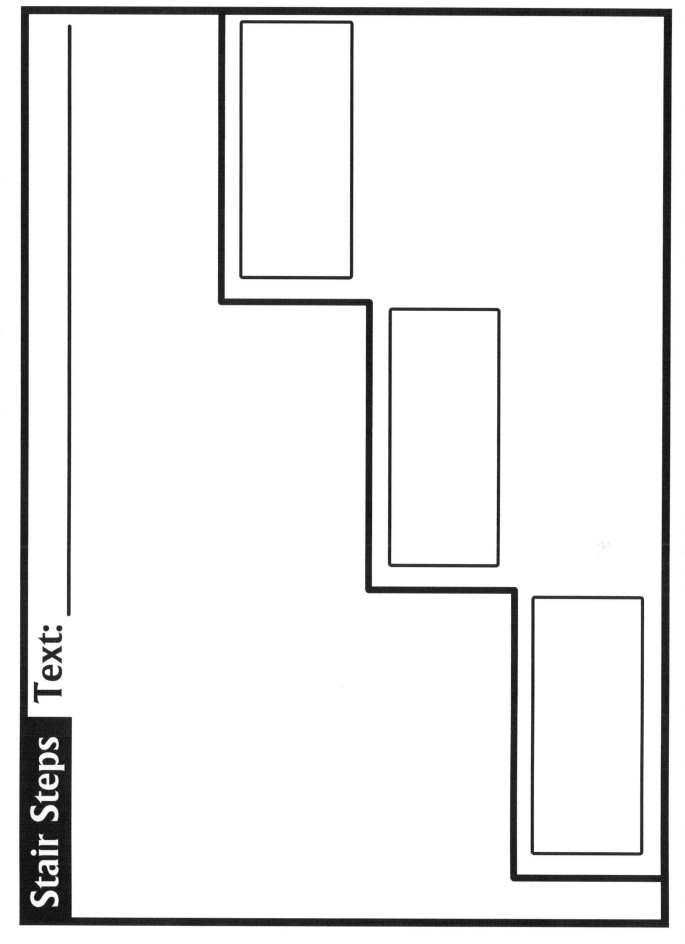

BETWEEN THE LINES

20

An alternative is to record the page & line number for reference to the textual evidence.

Between the Lines

Inference:	What the Text Said:
Frederick was an average guy. He wasn't glamourous.	... that was all another world to Frederick.
No one was concerned about the iceberg or the warnings.	Nothing more was said.
Walter Bedford was not viewed as highly as the day time bakers.	The honor of baking fancy pastry was reserved for the day shift.

Write a paragraph describing what you inferred from the textual evidence.

I learned a lot about how people were perceived. For example, Frederick's warnings were not treated with much urgency. Could it be because of his status? Similarly, Walter was stuck with the ordinary (not fancy) tasks.

Text: A Night to Remember

💣 **WARNING!**

Be careful to use the language of the common core standards with fidelity here. Overlooking this will create challenges as students move to the other standards.

The small size of the summary box results in careful consideration of what is really important. Small space = the information that really matters.

Between the Lines

Inference:

_____

_____

_____

_____

_____

_____

_____

_____

_____

What the Text Said:

_____

_____

_____

_____

_____

_____

Write a paragraph describing what you inferred from the textual evidence.

Text: _____

©2013 The Common Core Guidebook. Intended for classroom use only. May not be reproduced or distributed without permission.

QUOTE IT!

22

This organizer works well with basal or leveled readers on the same topic.

This chart makes a great large-scale reference chart for the class.

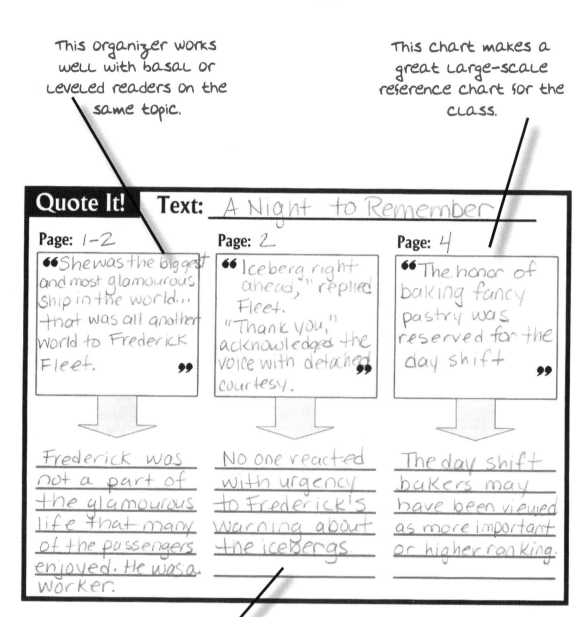

Quote It!   **Text:** A Night to Remember

Page: 1-2

"She was the biggest and most glamourous ship in the world... that was all another world to Frederick Fleet."

Frederick was not a part of the glamourous life that many of the passengers enjoyed. He was a worker.

Page: 2

"Iceberg right ahead," replied Fleet. "Thank you," acknowledged the voice with detached courtesy.

No one reacted with urgency to Frederick's warning about the icebergs.

Page: 4

"The honor of baking fancy pastry was reserved for the day shift"

The day shift bakers may have been viewed as more important or higher ranking.

Key Point

It is important to think-aloud as much as possible when you model this organizer. Students really need to see the connection between claims, inferences, & textual evidence.

©2013 The Common Core Guidebook. Intended for classroom use only. May not be reproduced or distributed without permission.

Quote It!

Text:

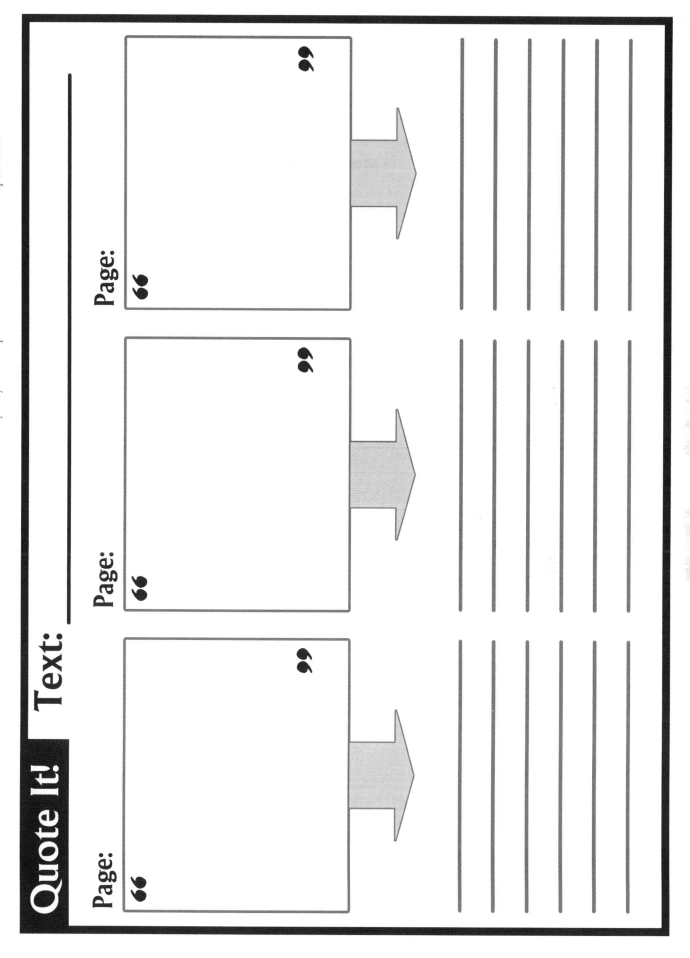

Page:

Page:

Page:

WHAT DO I NOTICE?

Great opportunity to talk about words we use to name text and the components that create larger chunks of text like sentences, lines, and paragraphs. Good link to RIS language.

This is an excellent activity to jigsaw. You can also let students complete what they notice on one side and switch papers to allow different students to look for the textual evidence to support the observations.

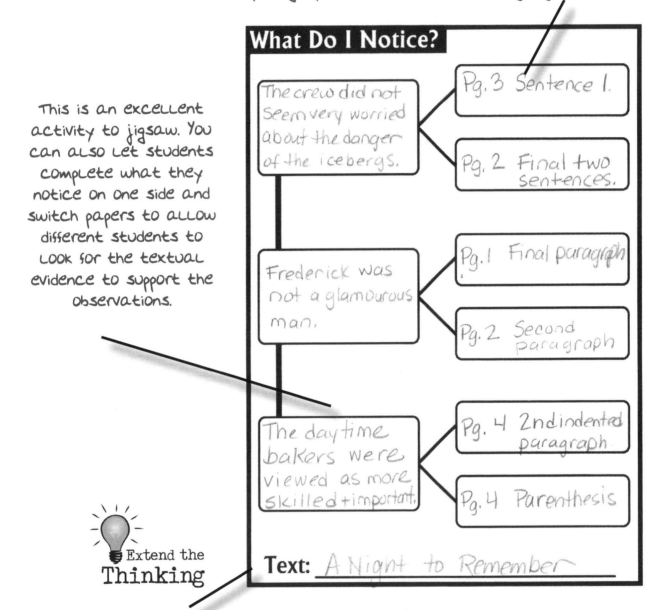

What Do I Notice?

The crew did not seem very worried about the danger of the icebergs.

Pg. 3 Sentence 1.

Pg. 2 Final two sentences.

Frederick was not a glamourous man.

Pg. 1 Final paragraph.

Pg. 2 Second paragraph

The day time bakers were viewed as more skilled + important.

Pg. 4 2nd indented paragraph.

Pg. 4 Parenthesis

Extend the Thinking

Text: A Night to Remember

An alternative is to read a selection & have your students complete colored sticky notes for what they notice. Then, use a different color sticky note for the textual evidence. Use a large wall or table and let students negotiate how the evidence and inferences fit together.

What Do I Notice?

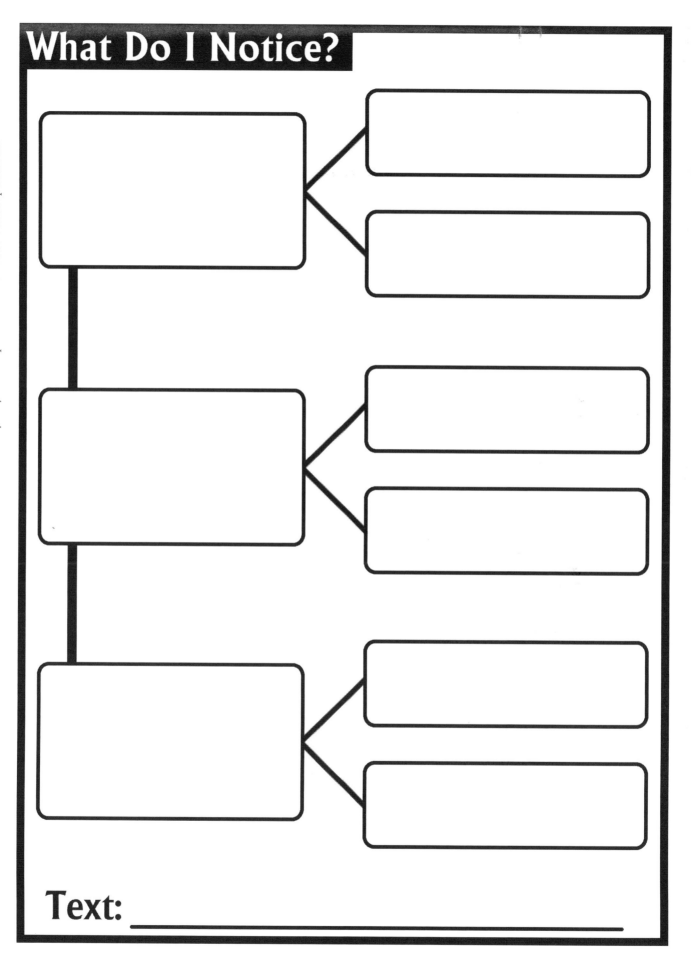

Text: _____

TE T-CHART

I like to use this as a quick formative assessment. A sheet of paper folded in half is a quick way for students to write their inferences & identify the textual evidence that supports them.

Extend the
Thinking

If you are ready to consider MLA, APA, or Chicago-style rules at your school, use the evidence side to introduce in-text citations in context.

Students have opportunity and space to include longer excerpts and quote text directly. Great foundation for the high school (9-12) version of this standard that requires more explicit citation and quoting of textual evidence.

consider assigning text excerpts & asking students to infer from those.

Textual Evidence T-Chart

Inference	Textual Evidence
Frederick was not glamourous like most of the ship's passengers.	"...it was already clear that she was not only the largest, but the most glamourous ship in the world. Even the passengers' dogs were glamourous... that was all another world to Frederick Fleet." Pg. 1-2
People did not seem to take Frederick's warnings about icebergs very seriously.	"Iceberg right ahead," replied Fleet. "Thank You," acknowledged the voice with detached courtesy. Nothing more was said. Pg. 2

Text: A Night to Remember

Textual Evidence T-Chart

Inference	Textual Evidence

Text: _____

©2013 The Common Core Guidebook. Intended for classroom use only. May not be reproduced or distributed without permission.

A Night to Remember
Walter Lord
ISBN: 978-0805077643

This text, suggested in the Common Core appendices, is classified as informational text. The book reads and is very much structured like a narrative account, so it will have a familiar feel for students. The events are retold based on interviews and firsthand sources. This text can easily be classified as historical fiction due to the narrative quality and creative liberties taken by the author. You will note that many of the Common Core informational text suggestions are historical fiction selections; informational text is not just a synonym for nonfiction text. A teachable moment for this text is to explore the nuances associated with classifying books as solely one genre or the other.

Artificial Sweeteners: Sugar-free, but at What Cost?
Holly Strawbridge
http://www.health.harvard.edu/blog/artificial-sweeteners-sugar-free-but-at-what-cost-201207165030

This informational text article examines the effects of a sugar-free diet supplemented with artificial sweeteners. Relying on data from the American Heart Association and the American Diabetes Association, this article is rich with quotes and hyperlinks to additional data.

Battle Heroes: Voices from Afghanistan
Allen Zullo
ISBN: 978-0545206426

This is a collection of ten firsthand accounts from soldiers stationed in Afghanistan. Gripping, emotional, and engaging, each tale offers numerous opportunities for readers to draw from textual evidence to make inferences.

Blood, Toil, Tears and Sweat: Address to Parliament on May 13th, 1940
Winston Churchill
http://www.winstonchurchill.org/learn/speeches/speeches-of-winston-churchill/92-blood-toil-tears-and-sweat
http://www.historyplace.com/speeches/churchill.htm

A text suggested in the Common Core appendices, this historical speech offers students multiple opportunities to consider how the ideas connect, which central ideas are developed, and the impact of specific word choices. The audio and print transcript is available. A great practice is to have students write annotations on the transcript to help guide them to ask questions while they read or listen to the text.

Four Perfect Pebbles: A Holocaust Story
Lila Perl
ISBN: 978-0380731886

This text traces the experiences of Marion Blumenthal and her family as they experience the horrors of the Holocaust. While the events are expectedly mature, the writing is appropriate for middle school readers. The personal narrative format offers a familiar style for students to understand. The book does not have the intensity of *Night* or *The Cage*, but the depth of information is profound and expansive.

Freedom's Children: Young Civil Rights Activists Tell Their Own Stories
Ellen S. Levine
ISBN: 978-0698118706

The Civil Rights Movement is told through the lens of young activists. Many of the young people featured in the text go on to become important fixtures in the movement. Experiences with segregation, violence, and basic human rights violations are at the center of this text, but addressed through a youthful, first-person viewpoint.

Getups
Published within *Wouldn't Take Nothing for My Journey Now*
Maya Angelou
ISBN: 978-0553569070

Getups is an essay that explores multiple themes. This text encourages critical thinking about social, family, and identity issues. In this essay, Angelou explains how her son grew to be embarrassed of his mother's eccentric appearance when he was a child. She shares how he requested that she wear cardigans to school like the other mothers and even limit her visits. Angelou explores how she responded, the lessons she took away, and offers multiple points for readers to make inferences about.

Harriet Tubman: Conductor on the Underground Railroad
Ann Petry
ISBN: 978-0064461818

Petry, the award-winning author of a children's book on Tubman's life, brings the same vivid descriptions and style to this version. Organized like a classic biography, this text provides an accessible account of the events in Harriet Tubman's life. Students are easily able to draw connections between Harriet as an individual and the events of this era. This text paints a dramatic image of life as a slave and the risks associated with trying to help others escape that life.

Narrative of the Life of Frederick Douglass, an American Slave, Written by Himself
Frederick Douglass
ISBN: 978-0486284996
Full electronic text is available from various online sources as well.
This text offers numerous passages where readers can make inferences about the character of Douglass and those around him. There are also a wide variety of instances where students can develop inferences with ample support for multiple conclusions.

Now is Your Time! The African-American Struggle for Freedom
Walter Dean Myers
ISBN: 978-0064461207
This collection of biographical vignettes is riveting and thought provoking. Short, yet powerful in content, each explores the life and struggle of a different African-American. Students will learn as much from the content as they do about analysis. This book pairs well with thematic units on courage and determination.

Scholastic Science World
www.scholastic.com/scienceworld
Science World includes short, easy articles that are often rich with data, facts, statistics, and a great deal of support. Students can read this magazine to locate textual evidence, analyze reasoning, and evaluate the strength of an argument. Similar to most of the other *Scholastic* publications, the content is engaging and diverse.

Shadow of the Titanic: The Extraordinary Stories of Those Who Survived
Andrew Wilson
ISBN: 978-1451671568
This text is based on the diaries, memories, letters, and interviews of the surviving members of the Titanic. Students can read specific chapters that follow individual survivors. The chapters chronicle how they remember that fateful day and how they coped after the event. Filled with colorful language, this text can be used in multiple ways to model the informational text standards.

The Greatest: Muhammad Ali
Walter Dean Myers
ISBN: 978-0590543439
This book presents the life of Ali, but touches on the social issues that were prominent at the time. Segregation and racism are front and center in this text. Myers' language and comfortable writing style make it easy for students to tackle complex topics such as these. The writing also lends itself to analysis in terms of style, grammar, and punctuation. Appositives, dependent clauses, and various quotations make this an excellent mentor text for how writers use language and syntax to communicate as well.

The Struggle to be an All-American Girl
Elizabeth Wong
Los Angeles Times, 1980 (Can be purchased from latimes.org online archive)
Full text is also easily found on the Internet.

This essay walks readers through the challenges that the author had growing up balancing the competing demands of being Chinese and her perceptions of being an American. Written from a teen perspective, the text offers a raw, honest perception of childhood desires and developing images of self. Students have several opportunities to draw inferences about the narrator and central ideas, as well as to make multiple extensions and connections.

Upfront Magazine
www.upfront.scholastic.com

Upfront is the brainchild of *Scholastic* and the *New York Times*. Teachers can order the magazine and access the articles online. Each issue comes with a teacher's guide and each article is lexiled and aligned to specific Common Core standards. There are also extension activities and resources for English Language Learners (ELL) as well.

Vincent Van Gogh: Portrait of an Artist
Jan Greenberg and Sandra Jordan
ISBN: 978-0440419174

This text can be used in numerous ways. The first chapter, *The Brabant Boy*, is an excellent starting point to explore the Textual Evidence standard. Students can make inferences about Vincent's birth, his parents' viewpoints toward having a child, and even discuss conflicting feelings that they can infer about the old versus the new Vincent. The rich description provides a great frame for exploring multiple conclusions and inferences.

Why we Worship "American Idol"
Thomas de Zengotita
Los Angeles Times, February 12, 2006
http://articles.latimes.com/2006/feb/12/opinion/op-zengotita12

This essay, written at the height of *American Idol's* popularity, explores why the show is so adored. The essay touches on the ideas of media influence, American interpretation of heroes, and the power of music. The article does a respectable job of balancing everyday concepts with engaging language to keep readers interested. Despite the playful title, this text is complex and requires a close read. The word choices vary immensely and students encounter terms such as: climactic, capitalist, spectators, flash-mobbing, excruciating, conventional, and articulated. Note: the article uses the word pornography and may not be a good choice for less mature students. Please preview the text carefully to make an appropriate choice for your students.

Central Ideas

"I can't understand why people are frightened of new ideas. I'm frightened of the old ones."
John Cage, composer

READING INFORMATIONAL TEXT STANDARD 2:
CENTRAL IDEAS

Sixth	Seventh	Eighth
Determine a central idea of a text and how it is conveyed through particular details; provide a summary of the text distinct from personal opinions or judgments.	Determine two or more central ideas in a text and analyze their development over the course of the text; provide an objective summary of the text.	Determine a central idea of a text and analyze its development over the course of the text, including its relationship to supporting ideas; provide an objective summary of the text.

GRADE LEVEL DIFFERENCES

This is one standard where sixth and eighth grade are almost identical, but seventh grade is the outlier. Sixth and eighth graders are expected to determine one central idea of an informational text and objectively summarize the text. Seventh graders are expected to determine at least two central ideas and objectively summarize the text.

The focus of the Central Ideas standard is twofold. Students are tasked with both determining what message the author is trying to relay to readers as well as being able to succinctly summarize that message. In one sense, the standard demands that students look carefully at the underlying ideas of a text. Students need to identify the central ideas, write about how they are developed, and then summarize what they read. The link between reading and asking students to write summaries of their reading is critical to deepening their understanding of a text. Research indicates that when anyone, adult or child, writes about their understanding of a text, their engagement increases and cognition about the text deepens (Tierney & Shanahan, 1996).

Mastery of this standard involves two key skills: the ability to determine central ideas and to objectively summarize a text. For students to arrive at mastery, they need to be able to:

► **Summarize text**

► **Recognize how to write objectively**

► **Identify a central idea or ideas**

► **Understand how central ideas are developed**

If a student can determine the central idea, but cannot write a summary about it, they have not mastered the standard. If the student can write a summary, but

it is not objective, they have not mastered the standard. A good analogy for conceptualizing this standard is to picture students playing the game of Operation™. Students have those tiny plastic tweezers and they are carefully attempting to pull out all of the wishbones and organs. Your goal is to help them learn how to remove those central parts and summarize what they are all about.

Avoid teaching that there is one central idea. Students should be able to identify that there can be multiple central ideas in a text. The focus for informational text is to ensure that students can analyze myriad forms of writing. Students should examine magazine articles, blog posts, website content, editorials, and historical documents. Be certain that they recognize that all writing contains central ideas. Students are analyzing what the author wants them to know and how the author worked to do this through details.

If you conceptualize the Common Core standards as progressive, you can see how the Textual Evidence standard is a precursor or simply a component that students need to understand before they can break those inferences into ideas and details. Understanding the Central Ideas standard requires a keen awareness of the Textual Evidence standard. The knowledge base builds with these two standards. As you explore the other standards, you will also see the strong connection and reliance on the Textual Evidence standard throughout each one. As students make meaning of text, they will always be responsible for identifying evidence that supports their thinking.

Common Core Buzzword

Notice the shift in language to the term: central ideas. The emphasis is to show that multiple ideas can be central to a text. Consider your personal reading. How often is a text really just about one central idea? Rarely.

1 Make a connection between what students have learned about the first standard (Textual Evidence) to the learning for the Central Ideas standard. *"Today we are going to talk more about textual evidence, but with a bit more detail. We already discussed how to find textual evidence to help support our inferences about a text. Today we will ask ourselves a new question: What is this text really about? We will try to limit it to one or two key ideas. These key ideas will be called central ideas. Once we decide what central idea or ideas the text is about, we will find textual evidence that supports the central idea."*

2 Select a documentary trailer for students to watch. See the suggested text list at the end of this chapter for sources of documentary trailers. I like using multimedia and film with students because this medium resonates with many of them. James Gee (2004) coined the term "affinity space" to describe a virtual or physical place where students learn informally. One of the most common communities or affinity spaces where students go to learn is YouTube. Learning through video tutorials is common with students. Using just a small slice of what is informally accepted by most young people as an appropriate medium tends to foster a higher level of early interest in any concept. Granted, this does not, by any means, qualify as creating an affinity space; it just offers a brief, nonthreatening connection to a modality of learning that most students welcome.

Extend the Thinking

Not a fan of documentaries? Consider picture books or fractured fairy tales. The goal for this stage is not yet about complex text. It's about accessible text.

3 After viewing one documentary trailer, lead a discussion about what the central ideas were in the documentary. Encourage students to share specific evidence from the documentary that helps support their ideas. *"How do you know?"*

4 Watch at least two more documentary trailers and use chart paper to record the name of the documentary, the central ideas, and evidence to support those central ideas.

5 Explain to students that they will use this same strategy when they read any informational text. Students will look for the central ideas and find specific evidence that helps support those central ideas.

1 **Select a news article for students to read from the *New York Times* (see suggested text list for the hyperlink).** If you have access to an actual set of newspapers, clip an article from that source or even select from a basal or newspaper-style anthology article for this lesson.

2 **Make a copy of the article for the students and one for yourself to display or project for your think-aloud.** If you have an interactive whiteboard, consider projecting the article on the screen and writing on the screen as you think out loud.

3 **As you read, underline key words and main ideas or list them on chart paper.** Talk with students about why you think specific ideas are important. Engage in discussions as needed about areas that you choose not to underline or write down. What helped you make that decision? Ask students to think about what they would underline or determine as most important.

4 **Continue to think out loud as you underline parts of the article, asking students to follow along and circle key words.** *"As I underline specific parts, I am asking myself if this is what is most important. Is this what the author wants me to remember? If the information does not seem to help me understand the article, I won't underline it. I am looking for the big ideas that I can think about and remember when I retell what this article is about to someone else."*

5 **Think out loud as you write a brief summary (less than 40 words) of what you read.** Depending on your class, you may want to encourage the students to write a summary with you or ask them to collaborate and create their own summaries.

6 **Be careful to point out that summaries do not include outside information based on our opinions.** Stress the need to be objective. If students struggle with the concept of objectivity, take a moment to build a short mini-lesson into your modeling, or introduce the concept in advance as a vocabulary preview to this lesson.

THE ORGANIZERS

Once you have explicitly introduced and modeled how to apply the strategies of the standard, now is the time to shift gears and provide students with multiple opportunities to practice the skill with their own reading in pairs, groups, and independently.

Students always need models, so each organizer has been completed based on *Geeks* by John Katz. This text is suggested within the Common Core appendices as an appropriate informational text under the reading strand. This particular text is used for each example under the Central Ideas standard for consistency and to offer the same book as a point of comparison for teachers.

1 Read (or reread) the introduction from *Geeks* with students. If you don't have a copy for each student, project the text so that all students can read it. Model how to complete the organizer using the samples that I have modeled next to each organizer or complete your own sample from the blank copy found in each section.

2 Once you model by explicitly completing the organizer yourself, your students will see the connection between the informational text and the organizer. You can provide blank copies of the organizer and allow students to select their own informational text, assign one from your class anthology, or select a title from the suggested book list within this chapter.

3 Students can complete the organizer when they read *any* informational text. This can be done as an assignment and can be repeated as many times as you want with any informational text that you choose. The sky is the limit! This allows for multiple opportunities to tailor the text to the student and maintain fidelity to the standard.

4 Once students have demonstrated mastery of the skill, don't stop using it. You want them to keep practicing. In the introduction of the book, I discussed the pitfalls of being a Checklist Teacher. Students need to keep perfecting their skill sets.

5 Reuse the same organizer, make it into an anchor chart, or post exemplars for students to reference later. You can add the organizer to a Central Ideas center, pair it with your school's reading incentive program to focus on Common Core skills with all reading activities, or use it daily as evidence of reading.

DEVELOPING IDEAS

Be certain to reinforce that informational text can have multiple central ideas. The main focus is on students tracing the development & the details used to structure those ideas.

Focus on different ideas throughout the course of the text or the evolution of just one idea.

38

Developing Ideas

Central Idea

> Despite adversity, being true to who you are can result in courage and success.

What did I learn about this idea?

... in the beginning?	... in the middle?	... in the end?
Geeks were isolated and treated poorly by jocks in middle & high school.	Geeks start to see that they are not really isolated. There is a secret society.	Geeks become self-proclaimed geeks and own who they are & their place in society.

What details did the author use over the course of the text?

Details used:	Details used:	Details used:
- Described this as a universal experience of geeks.	- Katz interview - The Rise of the Geeks article.	- Mentions great universities they attended. - Global economy 𝜋

Key Point

Remember: Each organizer needs to be explicitly modeled and completed with students. You want students to be able to use these autonomously. This will be difficult without explicit modeling with an accessible text.

©2013 The Common Core Guidebook. Intended for classroom use only. May not be reproduced or distributed without permission.

Developing Ideas

Central Idea

What did I learn about this idea?

...in the beginning?

...in the middle?

...in the end?

What details did the author use over the course of the text?

Details used:

Details used:

Details used:

CENTRAL IDEA WEB

40

This is another easy organizer for students to recreate on notebook paper.

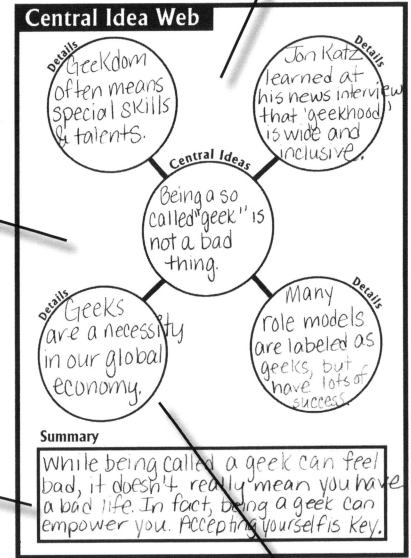

Central Idea Web

Details — Geekdom often means special skills & talents.

Details — Jon Katz learned at his news interview that "geekhood" is wide and inclusive.

Central Ideas — Being a so called "geek" is not a bad thing.

Details — Geeks are a necessity in our global economy.

Details — Many role models are labeled as geeks, but have lots of success.

Summary

While being called a geek can feel bad, it doesn't really mean you have a bad life. In fact, being a geek can empower you. Accepting yourself is key.

During your think-aloud, select some details that don't help to further the central ideas. Let students join you as you negotiate whether to include those details or not.

Small summary space demands a shorter summary so students get right to the point.

Key Point — Make the connection to the Central Ideas standard and the Textual Evidence standard.

Central Idea Web

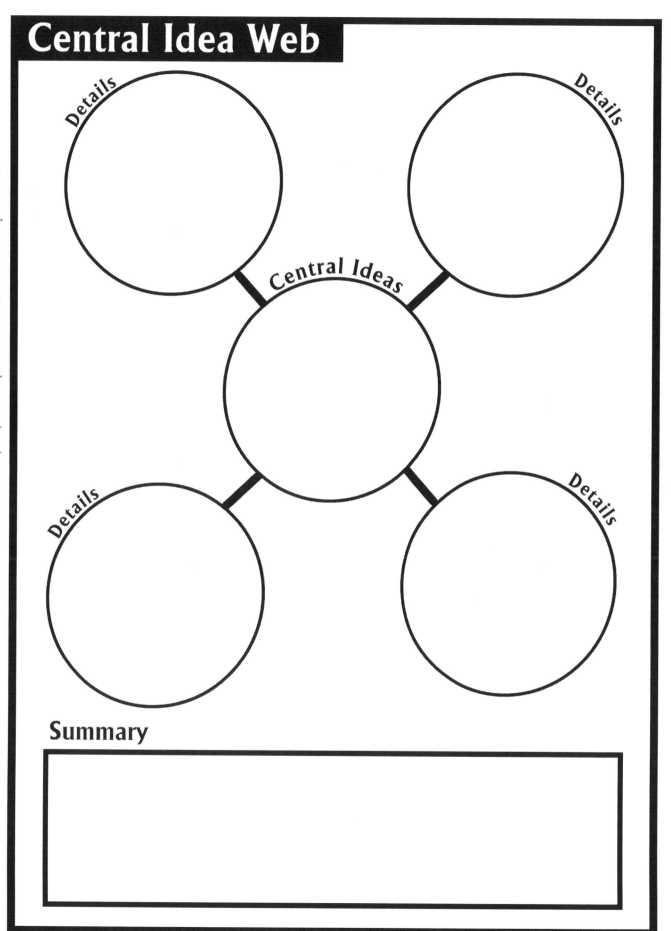

Details

Details

Central Ideas

Details

Details

Summary

©2013 The Common Core Guidebook. Intended for classroom use only. May not be reproduced or distributed without permission.

TWO CENTRAL IDEAS

Two Central Ideas is a requirement for 7th grade students.

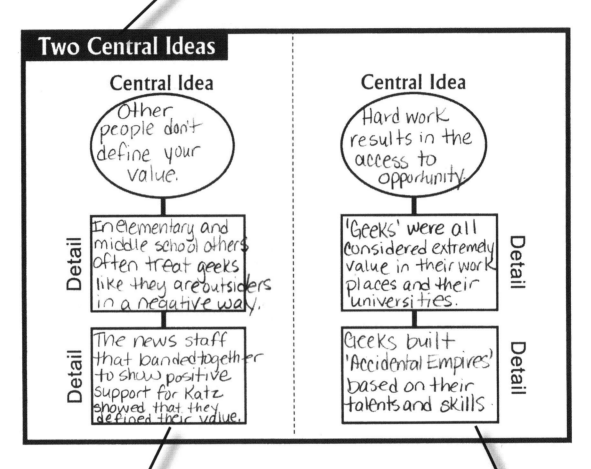

Two Central Ideas

Central Idea

Other people don't define your value.

Detail

In elementary and middle school others often treat geeks like they are outsiders in a negative way.

Detail

The news staff that banded together to show positive support for Katz showed that they defined their value.

Central Idea

Hard work results in the access to opportunity.

'Geeks' were all considered extremely value in their work places and their universities.

Detail

Geeks built 'Accidental Empires' based on their talents and skills.

Detail

Extend the
Thinking

A fun alternative is to use yellow sticky notes for the central ideas & blue or pink for the details. create a central ideas detail wall for one text.

Give students a set of details & have them determine which ones support the central ideas & which do not.

©2013 The Common Core Guidebook. Intended for classroom use only. May not be reproduced or distributed without permission.

Two Central Ideas

Central Idea

Detail

Detail

Central Idea

Detail

Detail

IDEA CYCLE

Great tie in to the
Literature (RL)
standard on theme.

Extend the
Thinking

A fun project is to ask
students to create
a presentation of the
central ideas in the
text. A movie, visual
display, or blog can
be used not only to
present the ideas, but
offer a narrative of
why the ideas were
selected.

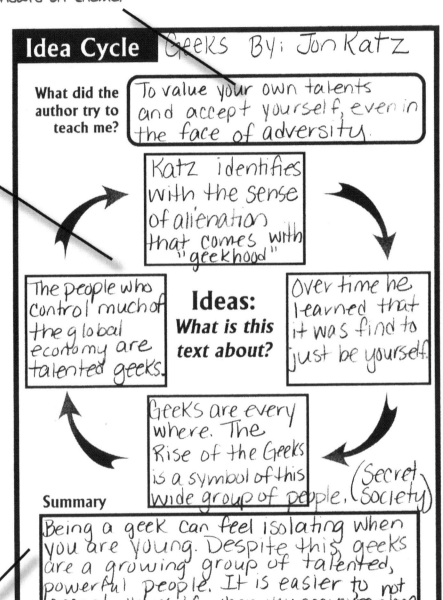

Idea Cycle   Geeks By: Jon Katz

What did the author try to teach me? To value your own talents and accept yourself, even in the face of adversity.

Katz identifies with the sense of alienation that comes with "geekhood"

Ideas: What is this text about?

The people who control much of the global economy are talented geeks.

Over time he learned that it was find to just be yourself.

Geeks are every where. The Rise of the Geeks is a symbol of this wide group of people. (Secret Society)

Summary

Being a geek can feel isolating when you are young. Despite this, geeks are a growing group of talented, powerful people. It is easier to not accept yourself when you see you're alone.

Small space = more
succinct summary

Let students present their
cycles & explain why they
chose the order that they did.

Idea Cycle

What did the author try to teach me?

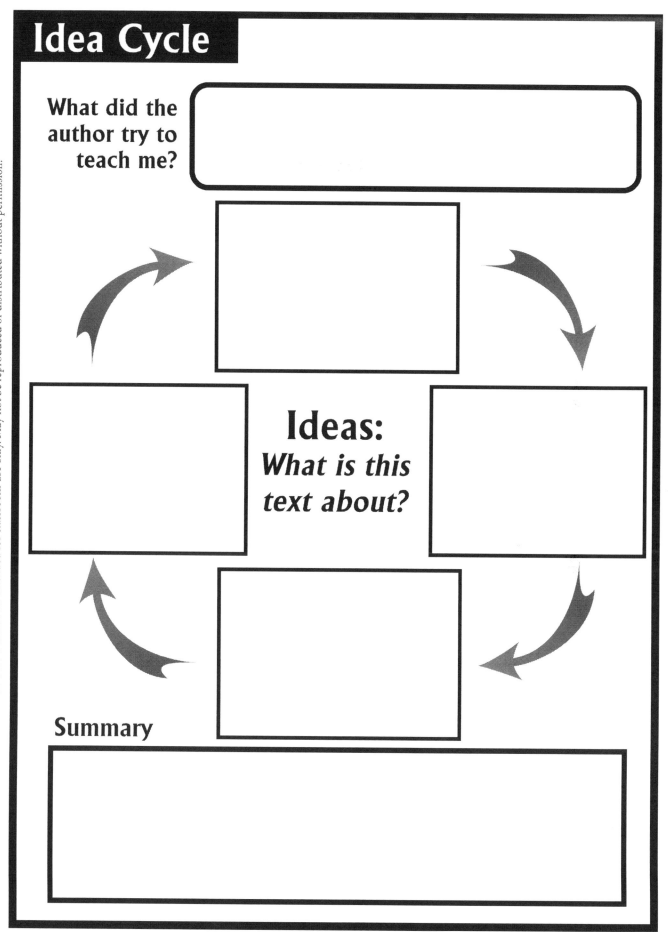

Ideas:
What is this text about?

Summary

©2013 The Common Core Guidebook. Intended for classroom use only. May not be reproduced or distributed without permission.

TEACH ME

WARNING! Students will struggle with this concept. I like to draw parallels between this standard & the messages or morals that they find in fairytale literature. what should you walk away knowing?

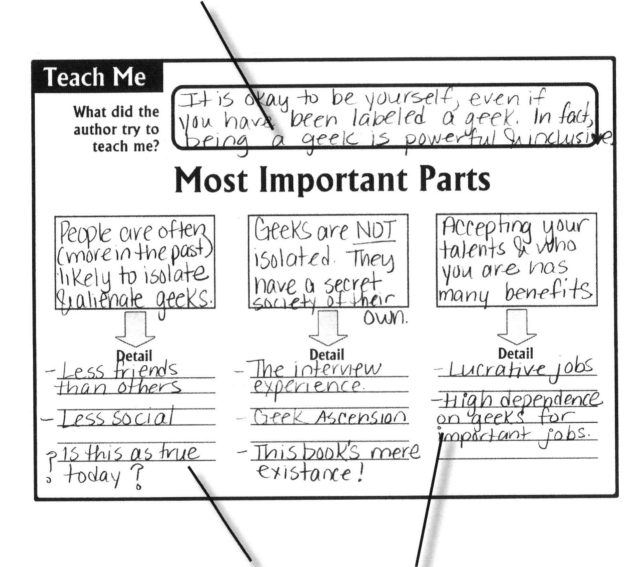

Teach Me

What did the author try to teach me?

It is okay to be yourself, even if you have been labeled a geek. In fact, being a geek is powerful & inclusive.

Most Important Parts

People are often (more in the past) likely to isolate & alienate geeks.

Geeks are NOT isolated. They have a secret society of their own.

Accepting your talents & who you are has many benefits

Detail
- Less friends than others
- Less social
- ? Is this as true today ?

Detail
- The interview experience.
- Geek Ascension
- This book's mere existance!

Detail
- Lucrative jobs
- High dependence on geeks for important jobs.

Teach student to question the text & content as they analyze.

Bullets work best here.

©2013 The Common Core Guidebook. Intended for classroom use only. May not be reproduced or distributed without permission.

Teach Me

What did the author try to teach me?

Most Important Parts

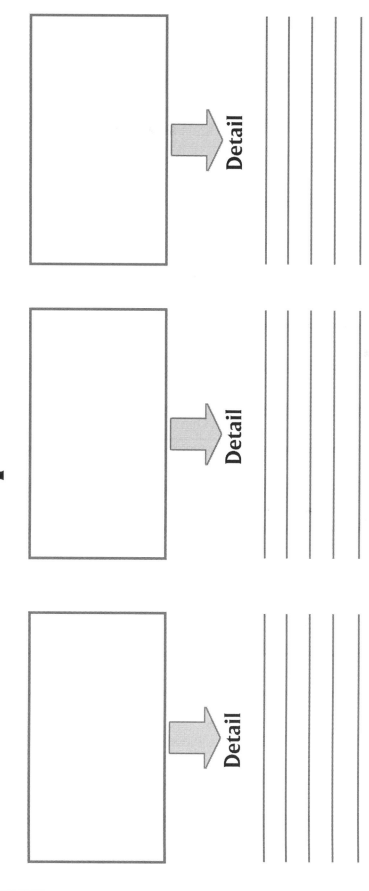

Detail

Detail

Detail

ANTHOLOGIES/BOOKS WITH MULTIPLE STORIES

I enjoy anthology collections for modeling the Central Ideas standard. These provide students with authentic collections of informational writing, often written for adults, but accessible to middle school students. These also provide great examples of real-life informational text that diverge from the typical expository or news writing that most students will already be familiar with. The *Best of Writing* series is an expansive example with multiple volumes. Popular ones that I have enjoyed using with students include collections on science, nature, travel, sports, and magazine writing. The *Chicken Soup* series is another flexible anthology choice. For about ten dollars, you can snag a collection of informational text essays reflective of what your students enjoy reading. This list is comprised of some of my favorite anthologies to use with middle school students. You can consider using these to find topics that interest you and your students and to promote engagement.

Boys Who Rocked the World: From King Tut to Bruce Lee
Michelle Roehm McCann
ISBN: 978-1582703312

Crafted with engaging word choices and fairly straightforward language, this text offers a wealth of biographical information on historical and contemporary male figures. The text is well suited for exploring central ideas and text structure. Readers can analyze the purpose of specific sections within the biographies or even use the individual chapters as models for organizing their own explanatory text and biographies. See also the female version by the same author: *Girls Who Rocked the World*.

Chicken Soup for the Soul: Teens Talk Middle School: 101 Stories of Life, Love, and Learning for Younger Teens
Jack Canfield, Mark Victor Hansen, Madeline Clapps, and Valerie Howlett
ISBN: 978-1935096269

This book is filled with over 100 (mostly) nonfiction accounts that all focus on one theme: middle school life. Each one offers an experience or central idea that many of your students can and will easily relate to. Preview all sections for inappropriate content before using.

Girls Who Rocked the World: Heroines from Joan of Arc to Mother Teresa
Michelle Roehm McCann and Amelie Welden
ISBN: 978-1582703022

Well suited to your struggling readers, this book shouts Girl Power on every page. This empowering read for preteen girls offers historical data and interesting facts about a wide variety of female heroines. The reading is fairly easy and is probably best suited for sixth graders and reluctant readers. This book is a great source when considering central ideas, relationships, and even text structure. See also the male version: *Boys Who Rocked the World* by the same author.

The Best American Essays of the Century (The Best American Series)
Joyce Carol Oates and Robert Atwan
ISBN: 978-0618155873

These essays offer a wide range of topics and varying reading levels. This text offers multiple opportunities for shared and independent reading. The strength of this text is in the diversity of language, organization, and style. This one text could be used multiple times to model and teach all of the informational text standards.

The Best American Travel Writing 2012
Jason Wilson and William Vollman
ISBN: 978-0547808970

This text offers a collection of informational essays ranging from six or seven pages to over twenty-five. This should not be assigned as a set to simply read independently. The variety of language and higher-level vocabulary also makes the essays in this text a good choice for the Word Play standard. Close reading can easily be taught through these types of essays, offering multiple opportunities for shared reading, independent reading, and increasing text complexity among students. The strength of this text is in the diversity of language, organization, and style. This one text could be used multiple times to model and extend almost every informational text standard.

Teens Write Through It: Essays from Teens Who've Triumphed over Trouble
Fairview Press
ISBN: 978-1577490838

This collection of essays offers a powerful example of published teen writing. Each essay is crafted to share the experiences and lesson or central ideas taken away from the experiences. The authentic voices and easily relatable topics are effective at engaging preteen and teen readers.

CONTEMPORARY/GUIDES

The 7 Habits of Highly Effective Teens
Sean Covey
ISBN: 978-0684856094

The 7 Habits of Highly Effective Teens brings the same style of writing that adults have come to expect from author Sean Covey. Covey applies his principles of the seven habits to teens, but with a focus on issues that they face and value. Witty and engaging, the text offers steps to improve self-image, resist peer pressure, and set goals. While this is technically not an anthology or collection of essays, it can be used in the same way. Each chapter or habit can even stand alone as an individual piece, making this text useful as a collection of essays or as a single piece.

The Teen's Guide to World Domination: Advice on Life, Liberty, and the Pursuit of Awesomeness

Josh Shipp

ISBN: 978-0312641542

Filled with wit and a dose of sarcasm, this book is an entertaining read. The word choices and clever analogies offer examples of organization and writer's craft. This text is one of the few examples where simple, teen-relevant content is presented in a fun way, but still offers the reader a great deal to examine in terms of style, message, voice, and organization. I would reserve this for my eighth graders, but it can be read by any grade level. Preview carefully for sensitive content and word choices.

What Do You Really Want? How to Set a Goal and Go for It! A Guide for Teens

Beverly K. Bachel

ISBN: 978-1575420851

This 130-page text is a how-to guide for preteens and teens. Reflective of the actual type of informational text reading that adults do, this selection is about self-improvement. Teens don't need prior knowledge or subject-area content to relate to the topic. I would recommend this book for the reluctant reader in your class. The student that typically asks (with a scowl): *"why are we reading this?"* when you present your classical favorites or historically-based texts will enjoy this book.

HISTORICAL TEXT

A Long Way Gone: The True Story of a Child Soldier

Ishmael Beah

ISBN: 978-0-374-53126-3

This emotional story recounts Ishmael Beah's experiences as a boy being recruited into the national army to serve as a child soldier. The text traces his early experiences in Sierra Leone in the 1990s, a period known for its brutality and violence, his time in a rehabilitation center, and reentry into society. The text is conversational and easy to read, but the images and experiences can be challenging for young readers. This is a text to preview carefully before sharing with your students. There may be sections that you want to skip or introduce delicately.

A Night to Remember

Walter Lord

ISBN: 978-0805077643

This text, suggested in the Common Core appendices, is classified as informational text. The book reads and is very much structured like a narrative account, so it will have a familiar feel for students. The events are retold based on interviews and firsthand sources.

This text can easily be classified as historical fiction due to the narrative quality and creative liberties taken by the author. You will note that many of the Common Core informational text suggestions are historical fiction selections. Informational text is not just a synonym for nonfiction text. A teachable moment for this text is to explore the nuances associated with classifying books as solely one genre or the other.

Days of Jubilee: The End of Slavery in the United States
Patricia McKissack and Frederick McKissack
ISBN: 978-0590107648

While the signing of the Emancipation Proclamation is historically referred to as the end of slavery, sadly, it was not. Many slaves waited years for their freedom. This hopeful day became known as the Day of Jubilee. Multiple perspectives are included based on first-hand source documents. This is an excellent match for social studies units that explore the Civil War or The Civil Rights Movement. This text offers a wide variety of organizational structures. Students can examine sections to determine if they are organized to describe, sequence, or compare and contrast ideas, events, or individuals. This text is historically accurate, yet accessible for all readers.

Escape: Children of the Holocaust
Allan Zullo
978-0545099295

This historical informational text is a collection of Holocaust survivors' experiences as children in Germany. Presented as memoirs, each section chronicles the events of the Holocaust from a personal perspective. Since the Holocaust is taught in most social studies curriculums in middle school, this text offers a strong connection to what students will be learning about, but paints a very real face on those experiences.

Freedom Walkers: The Story of the Montgomery Bus Boycott
Russell Freedman
ISBN: 978-0823421954

This text combines personal recollections and historical accounts of the Montgomery Bus Boycott. Legendary civil rights activists such as Parks, King, and Colvin are included in a photo-essay format.

Freedom's Children: Young Civil Rights Activists Tell Their Own Stories
Ellen S. Levine
ISBN: 978-0698118706

The Civil Rights Movement is told through the lens of young activists. Many of the young people featured in the text go on to become important fixtures in the movement. Experiences with segregation, violence, and basic human rights violations are at the center of this text, but addressed through a youthful, first-person viewpoint.

Harlem Stomp! A Cultural History Of The Harlem Renaissance
Laban Carrick Hill
ISBN: 978-0316034241

This book shows the pride and responsibility that emerged during the Harlem Renaissance. The text traces the violence of the 1919 'Red Summer' to the subsequent musical, visual, and written art explosion of the Renaissance. This text is filled with archival magazine covers, photographs, and posters.

Narrative of the Life of Frederick Douglass, an American Slave, Written by Himself
Frederick Douglass
ISBN: 978-0486284996
Full electronic text is available from various online sources as well.

This text offers numerous passages where readers can make inferences about the character of Douglass and those around him. There are also a wide variety of instances where students can develop inferences with ample support for multiple conclusions.

Sacajawea
Joseph Bruchac
ISBN: 978-0152064556

This tale traces the life of Sacajawea through the alternating voices of Sacajawea and William Clark. Original excerpts from Clark's diaries enhance the facts and narrative feel. This text is excellent for studying most of the informational text standards.

The Great Fire
Jim Murphy
ISBN: 978-0439203074

This informational text recounts the 1871 fire that destroyed much of Chicago. Murphy's text, created from primary sources, combines factual details with colorful word choices and suspense often reserved for fiction. The text includes multiple accounts that offer numerous viewpoints in one book. Sepia images, newspaper clippings, and photos are found on most pages.

Young, Black, and Determined: A Biography of Lorraine Hansberry
Patricia McKissack and Frederick McKissack
ISBN: 978-0823413003

The McKissacks have a long history of crafting biographies that celebrate African-American and minority figures. With a blend of colorful language and important facts, the text presents the seldom-told story of Hansberry's contribution to the American canon and her struggles in life. This text offers numerous opportunities for students to connect ideas, events, and individuals while considering author's viewpoint and word choices.

ONLINE/DIGITAL TEXT

35 Ancient Pyramids Discovered in Sudan Necropolis
Owen Jarvis

http://www.livescience.com/26903-35-ancient-pyramids-sudan.html

This article is a quick and simple text to read. Despite this, there are numerous opportunities to close read and consider the evidence, claims, and arguments that the author is making. Students have a wealth of informational text features such as photographs, related hyperlinks, and images to navigate as they read.

Blood, Toil, Tears and Sweat: Address to Parliament on May 13th, 1940
Winston Churchill

http://www.winstonchurchill.org/learn/speeches/speeches-of-winston-churchill/92-blood-toil-tears-and-sweat
http://www.historyplace.com/speeches/churchill.htm

A text suggested in the Common Core appendices, this historical speech offers students multiple opportunities to consider how the ideas connect, which central ideas are developed, and the impact of specific word choices. The audio and print transcript is available. A great practice is to have students write annotations on the transcript to help guide them to ask questions while they read or listen to the text.

Conversations with America
Julia Alvarez

http://weekendamerica.publicradio.org/display/web/2008/11/01/conversations_alvarez/

This is possibly the shortest text included on the suggested text list. This brief essay-style article features Alvarez explaining what the right to vote means to her. She uses her own experiences and quotes to voice her feelings about voting. This piece is an excellent companion for any social studies unit on voting rights or the electoral process.

How Birds Got Their UV Vision
Livescience
Tanya Lewis

http://news.discovery.com/animals/how-birds-uv-got-vision-130211.htm

This article is an easier article to read overall, but includes a wide variety of new science vocabulary words that students can use context clues to make meaning of. This text has multiple features such as images, related hyperlinks, and subheadings.

Pesticides Dropping in the Groundwater?
Jessica Marshall

http://dsc.discovery.com/news/2008/10/27/pesticides-groundwater.html

As is consistent with most *Discovery* news articles, this piece is filled with data and statistics. This is a true news story at its core, but it is easy to manage and accessible online. Students can read expert quotations, images, and links to similar stories. This text is useful for all of the informational text standards and could easily be revisited when modeling new strategies.

Reading, Writing, and Video Games

http://www.nytimes.com/2013/03/17/sunday-review/reading-writing-and-video-games.html

There are few middle school students that don't have an interest in or have friends that have an interest in video games. In this article, the author looks at how video game use has changed since the advent of nostalgic Atari™ games. The article explores the ways that technology is and can be used in school.

Connections & Relationships

"A book is not an isolated being: it is a relationship, an axis of innumerable relationships."

Jorge Luis Borges, author

READING INFORMATIONAL TEXT STANDARD 3:
CONNECTIONS & RELATIONSHIPS

Sixth	Seventh	Eighth
Analyze in detail how a key individual, event, or idea is introduced, illustrated, and elaborated in a text (e.g., through examples or anecdotes).	Analyze the interactions between individuals, events, and ideas in a text (e.g., how ideas influence individuals or events, or how individuals influence ideas or events).	Analyze how a text makes connections among and distinctions between individuals, ideas, or events (e.g., through comparisons, analogies, or categories).

GRADE LEVEL DIFFERENCES

This is one standard where the wording is different for each grade level, but the core skills still remain virtually the same. Each grade level is tasked with looking for relationships and explaining how they are established within the text.

56

Standard three is one of the most misunderstood Common Core standards. Many people see the word connection and fall back to the idea of text-text or text-world connections. The Connections & Relationships standard requires students to consider relationships between ideas, people, and events within the text. A simple way to think about this is to consider that students are making connections between the nouns in the text. What does one thing have to do with the other? How are two nouns related? Students are thinking about the relationships that they perceive and recognize. This demands the close reading of a text and the ability to make some judgment calls. Connections made by students will be diverse and varied.

So what exactly is a relationship? What does connection mean? Identifying connections is about looking at how two things interact. These interactions typically come in one of the following forms (but are definitely not limited to these):

- ▶ **Cause/Effect**

- ▶ **Problem/Solution**

- ▶ **Compare/Contrast or Similarities/Differences**

- ▶ **Sequence of Events**

- ▶ **Analogies**

- ▶ **Part Influencing Whole**

- ▶ **One Person/Big Event**

- ▶ **Big Event/One Person**

While most of these forms should seem familiar, the two forms that will be the least familiar are the two forms that

the Common Core standards explicitly discuss. These are the last two listed: One Person/Big Event and Big Event/One Person. Each of these is really a subset of Cause/Effect.

One Person/Big Event is when students make a connection between how one person influenced a larger event. Often found in historical text, these relationships are characterized in the Common Core standards as an individual influencing an event. Examples might include the relationship between Rosa Parks and the bus boycotts or the relationship between Abraham Lincoln and the Civil War.

Big Event/One Person is the inverse causal relationship of One Person/Big Event. This is where students consider how a broader event influences an individual person or groups of people. An example might include the relationship between the Holocaust and Elie Wiesel.

When students work on Text Structure (standard five), they will begin to look at how entire sections of text are organized in these same ways. For the Connections & Relationships standard students are simply tasked with pulling out events, individuals, and ideas and looking for these relationships and how they are developed.

Key Point

While students do need to make their own decisions about individuals, ideas, and events, do not center your instruction just on the connection. Focus on the evidence that supports and explains each connection.

1 Open with the idea that there are relationships and connections all around us. *"Everything is connected or related in some way. You can literally make a connection between almost any two ideas, individuals, or events."*

2 Establish that connections don't always have to be perceived in the exact same way. *"Everyone can find different connections, too. What I see may not be what you see. What matters is that you can look for multiple connections and explain the relationships that you see."*

3 Explain that there are some common relationships between ideas, people, and events. I use eight different relationships with my students (see anchor chart).

4 Create your own chart with the different ideas (choose a few or share them all).

5 Go through the list of relationship types and share a connection that you can make between real people, events, or ideas and ask for volunteers to do the same. *"In social studies we learned about Watergate. Because of the scandal, President Richard Nixon had to resign. So I just made a Cause/Effect connection about Richard Nixon. This could also be considered a Big Event that impacted One Person. Relationships overlap and so do the categories. Can anyone think of any other relationships that we could describe here?"*

RI 3: Connections & Relationships

Big Event _influences_→ One Person

One Person _influences_→ Big Event

Problem _that needs a_→ Solution

Cause _of a specific_→ Effect

Part _of a larger_→ Whole

Similarities _and_→ Differences

Analogies — One set of items shows the relationship between another set

Sequence of Events — Chronological Steps

58

1 **Select an informational text to read aloud.** Students should have their own copies or be able to access the text through an overhead or interactive whiteboard.

2 **As you read, tell students that you are going to look for:**

- ▶ **Individuals**
- ▶ **Events**
- ▶ **Ideas**

3 **Assign each category a color sticky note. For example:**

- ▶ **Individuals (yellow)**
- ▶ **Events (blue)**
- ▶ **Ideas (pink)**

4 **As you read aloud, stop when you get to an individual, idea, or event.** Discuss it and write it down on the corresponding color sticky note. Stick the notes on the board or in a visible place for all students.

5 **After you have read the piece, tell students that you want to see if they can make connections between any of the ideas, events, or individuals.** Think out loud as you begin pairing them together, explaining the relationship as you go. I like to let students move the sticky notes around.

6 **Repeat this process to create an anchor chart. This time focus on *one* type of connection. I like to use One Person/Big Event.** This is often easy to understand, yet powerful. Challenge your students to think of individuals that they have read about who have influenced a larger event. Add these ideas to one anchor chart for future reference.

RI3: Connections & Relationships

One Person ──influences a──▶ Big Event

1. Rosa Parks — Civil Right Movement through the bus boycotts
2. Adolf Hitler — Holocaust & the death of innocent people
3. Steve Jobs — Digital Communication
4. King James — The wording and printing of the contemporary bible.
5. Henry Ford — Transformation of the transportation industry
6. Abraham Lincoln — Trajectory of human rights for African Americans
7. Thomas Edison — Widespread use of electricity in homes

THE ORGANIZERS

Once you have explicitly introduced and modeled how to apply the strategies of the standard, now is the time to shift gears and provide students with multiple opportunities to practice the skill with their own reading in pairs, groups, and independently.

Students always need models, so each organizer has been completed based on *Geeks* by John Katz. This text is suggested within the Common Core appendices as an appropriate informational text under the reading strand. If you used the introduction from *Geeks* before with the Central Ideas standard, this will be very simple to model. Refer back to what you read in the introduction and talk about the content. Students can now easily focus on how the organizers work. This particular text is used for each example under Connections & Relationships for consistency and to offer the same book as a point of comparison for teachers.

1 Read (or reread) the introduction from *Geeks* with students. If you don't have a copy for each student, project the text so that all students can read it. Model how to complete the organizer using the samples that I have modeled next to each organizer or complete your own sample from the blank copy found in each section.

2 Once you model by explicitly completing the organizer yourself, your students will see the connection between the informational text and the organizer. You can provide blank copies of the organizer and allow students to select their own informational text, assign one from your class anthology, or select a title from the suggested book list within this chapter.

3 Students can complete the organizer when they read *any* informational text. This can be done as an assignment and can be repeated as many times as you want with any informational text that you choose. The sky is the limit! This allows for multiple opportunities to tailor the text to the student and maintain fidelity to the standard.

4 Once students have demonstrated mastery of the skill, don't stop using it. You want them to keep practicing. In the introduction of the book, I discussed the pitfalls of being a Checklist Teacher. Students need to keep perfecting their skill sets.

5 Reuse the same organizer, make it into an anchor chart, or post exemplars for students to reference later. You can add the organizer to a Connections & Relationships center, pair it with your school's reading incentive program to focus on Common Core skills with all reading activities, or use it daily as evidence of reading.

IDEA SORT

Extend the Thinking

I like to write the ideas, events, & people on index cards & lay them out like a Memory™ game. Let students uncover & defend connections.

Idea Sort

Ideas, Events, and Individuals

"The Other"	"Self-proclaimed geeks"	≠ friends
"Accidental Empires"	Secret Society	Bullying
"Lucrative Jobs"	Being called a geek	Top Universities
"Geek Ascension"	Superior technology abilities & skills	Mr. Katz on the local news

Negatives	Transformation	Acceptance
Category #1	Category #2	Category #3
1. "The Other"	1. "Geek Ascension"	1. Self proclaimed geeks
2. ≠ friends	2. "Secret Society"	2. Top universities
3. Bullying	3. Mr. Katz on news	3. "Lucrative jobs"
4. Being called a geek.	4. Superior tech skills	4. "Accidental empires"

Students are basically completing an open sort to classify & categorize.

You will be amazed at the diversity of categories that your students will define.

The Common Core Guidebook, 6-8: Informational Text Lessons

©2013 The Common Core Guidebook. Intended for classroom use only. May not be reproduced or distributed without permission.

Idea Sort

Ideas, Events, and Individuals

Category #1

1. _____
2. _____
3. _____
4. _____

Category #2

1. _____
2. _____
3. _____
4. _____

Category #3

1. _____
2. _____
3. _____
4. _____

IF . . . THEN

WARNING! Students will struggle with such open-ended choices. Scaffold & think-aloud to help students fill in those blanks & move to independence.

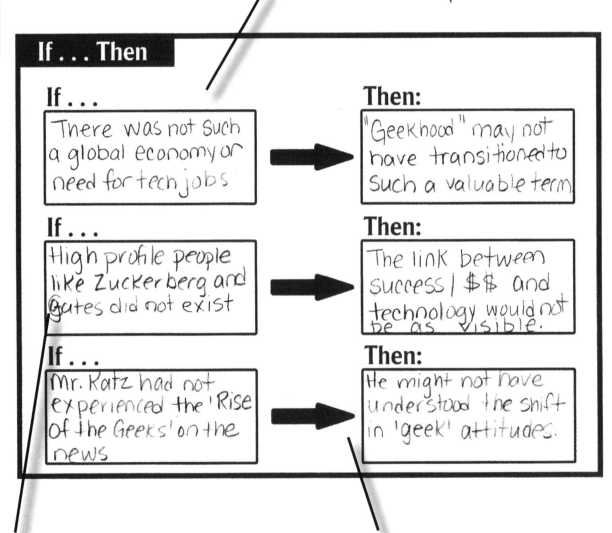

If . . . Then

If . . .
There was not such a global economy or need for tech jobs

Then:
"Geekhood" may not have transitioned to such a valuable term

If . . .
High profile people like Zuckerberg and Gates did not exist

Then:
The link between success/$$ and technology would not be as visible.

If . . .
Mr. Katz had not experienced the 'Rise of the Geeks' on the news

Then:
He might not have understood the shift in 'geek' attitudes.

This organizer is a great choice for social studies, historical events, & science experiment outcomes.

This pairs well with Standard RI5: Text Structure. Cause/effect is a major type of organization used with informational text.

©2013 The Common Core Guidebook. Intended for classroom use only. May not be reproduced or distributed without permission.

If . . . . Then

If . . . .

Then:

If . . . .

Then:

If . . . .

Then:

CONNECTION?

This is my favorite organizer for this standard. Students get to determine the connections & decide whether to use ideas, events, or individuals.

Connection?

Bullys and Jocks in middle and high school.	← They helped promote the idea that 'geeks' were bad or lesser people.	Geek as an insult or put down.
Lucrative jobs and excellent universities	The need for geeks helped change their value + status	Accidental Empires of so-called geeks
Mr. Katz on news & the "Rise of Geeks" article about him	Higher profile & connection resulted in self acceptance of word : geek.	Geekhood, Secret Society, Self proclaimed geeks, Greek Ascension

Students will be drawn to ideas rather than to individuals or events when they have a higher depth of knowledge of the text.

This makes a quick & easy assessment.

©2013 The Common Core Guidebook. Intended for classroom use only. May not be reproduced or distributed without permission.

Connection?

COMPARE IDEAS, EVENTS, AND INDIVIDUALS

I modeled this organizer using 3 major events from the introduction of Geeks. The book itself explores a much broader set of relationships & ideas.

Short on copies? This is a fast & easy organizer for students to recreate.

66

Compare Ideas, Events, and Individuals

Idea **Geek label**
-Very negative in MS & HS
- Shifted to a source of pride
- 'Geek Ascension'
-Secret Society

Saw that some looked at geeks negatively, but many did not!

Mixed experiences

Individual **Jon Katz**
- Successful
- Promoted & helped 'Geekhood' to be okay
-Connected & mentored others.

Everything changed for Jon's view of himself as a geek after that interview.

Felt old feelings of being a geek, but saw the power of geeks collectively.

Event **News Interview**

Venn diagrams feel comfortable & familiar to students.

WARNING! Some students will struggle with finding one idea, event, and individual. Allow flexibility for different combinations and groupings.

©2013 The Common Core Guidebook. Intended for classroom use only. May not be reproduced or distributed without permission.

Compare Ideas, Events, and Individuals

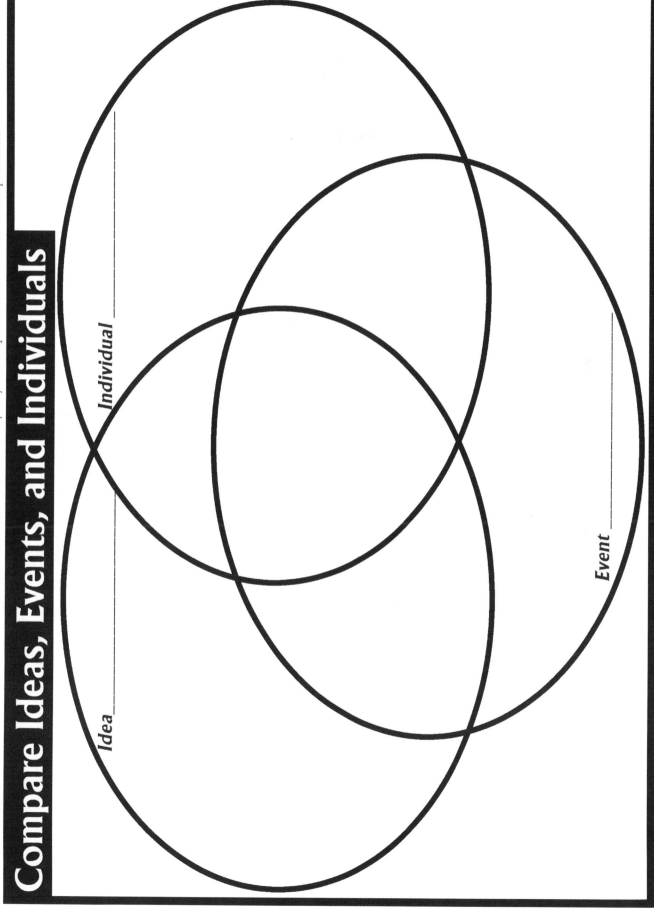

Individual

Idea

Event

Connections can be made when reading any informational text. Historical topics tend to offer the most lucid connections for students, as there are multiple events, ideas, and people to draw from. Most of the books on this list are historical for that reason.

HISTORICAL TEXT

A Night to Remember
Walter Lord
ISBN: 978-0805077643
This text, suggested in the Common Core appendices, is classified as informational text. The book reads and is very much structured like a narrative account, so it will have a familiar feel for students. The events are retold based on interviews and firsthand sources. This text can easily be classified as historical fiction due to the narrative quality and creative liberties taken by the author. You will note that many of the Common Core informational text suggestions are historical fiction selections. Informational text is not just a synonym for nonfiction text. A teachable moment for this text is to explore the nuances associated with classifying books as solely one genre or the other.

A Young People's History of the United States: Columbus to the War on Terror
Howard Zinn and Rebecca Stefoff
ISBN: 978-1583228692
Zinn offers a perspective of American history that is rarely communicated by textbooks. He challenges many of the dominant narratives and accepted versions of historical events, making this a text that requires a critical eye and which is worthy of close analysis.

Amelia Lost: The Life and Disappearance of Amelia Earhart
Candace Fleming
ISBN: 978-0375841989
This text chronicles Earhart's life and the circumstances of her mysterious disappearance. The text is engaging and provides a wealth of details and central ideas to consider.

Blood, Toil, Tears and Sweat: Address to Parliament on May 13th, 1940
Winston Churchill

http://www.winstonchurchill.org/learn/speeches/speeches-of-winston-churchill/92-blood-toil-tears-and-sweat
http://www.historyplace.com/speeches/churchill.htm

A text suggested in the Common Core appendices, this historical speech offers students multiple opportunities to consider how the ideas connect, which central ideas are developed, and the impact of specific word choices. The audio and print transcript is available. A great practice is to have students write annotations on the transcript to help guide them to ask questions while they read or listen to the text.

Dear Miss Breed: True Stories of the Japanese American Incarceration During World War II and a Librarian Who Made a Difference
Joanne Oppenheim
ISBN: 978-0439569927

Dear Miss Breed is a stirring account of World War II injustices. The text follows the experiences of a group of Japanese-Americans who were interned during the war in 1942. The text unfolds through a series of letters sent to San Diego librarian Clara Breed, archival materials, and interviews with the letters' grown-up authors. Oppenheim encourages readers to interrogate primary sources and critically examine documents from this era on their own. The author positions herself as an advocate for critical analysis and actively challenging the dominant narrative presented about World War II.

Escape: Children of the Holocaust
Allan Zullo
ISBN: 978-0545099295

This emotional informational text is a collection of Holocaust survivors' experiences as children in Germany. Since the Holocaust is taught in most social studies curriculums in middle school, this text offers a strong connection to what students will be learning about, but paints a very real face on those experiences.

Freedom Walkers: The Story of the Montgomery Bus Boycott
Russell Freedman
ISBN: 978-0823421954

This text combines personal recollections and historical accounts of the Montgomery Bus Boycott. Legendary civil rights activists such as Parks, King, and Colvin are included in a photo-essay format.

Harriet Tubman: Conductor on the Underground Railroad
Ann Petry
ISBN: 978-0064461818

Petry, the award-winning author of a children's book on Tubman's life, brings the same vivid descriptions and style to this version. Organized like a classic biography, this text provides an accessible account of the events in Harriet Tubman's life. Students are easily able to draw connections between Harriet as an individual and the events of this era. This text paints a dramatic image of life as a slave and the risks associated with trying to help others escape that life.

Narrative of the Life of Frederick Douglass, an American Slave, Written by Himself
Frederick Douglass
ISBN: 978-0486284996
Full electronic text is available from various online sources as well.
This text offers numerous passages where readers can make inferences about the character of Douglass and those around him. There are also a wide variety of instances where students can develop inferences with ample support for multiple conclusions.

Kids on Strike!
Susan Bartoletti
ISBN: 978-0618369232
This is a fairly easy read that explores the idea of child exploitation. Drawing historically from the Industrial Revolution era, this account of children in the workplace includes gripping images and thought-provoking text.

Red Scarf Girl: A Memoir of the Cultural Revolution
Ji-li Jiang
ISBN: 978-0061667718
This true story traces the experiences of 12-year-old Ji-li Jiang. Growing up in Communist China, she recounts the reign of Mao Ze-dong. Ripped apart from her father and driven into a life of terror, Ji-li faces adversity and struggle. This moving memoir will introduce students to a side of Chinese history and life that most will be unaware of while offering the perspective of a person their own age.

Sacajawea
Joseph Bruchac
ISBN: 978-0152064556
This tale traces the life of Sacajawea through the alternating voices of Sacajawea and William Clark. Original excerpts from Clark's diaries enhance the facts and narrative feel. This text is excellent for studying most of the informational text standards.

Surviving Hitler: A Boy in Nazi Death Camps
Andrea Warren
ISBN: 978-0060007676
Warren crafts a powerful piece that includes photographs and details that recount the experiences of Holocaust survivor Jack Mandelbaum. The text traces his experiences from the age of 12. Readers experience his misconceptions and shifts in understanding of this historical period. Warren does an excellent job of capturing a youthful view of events merged with the nightmarish suffering of the era.

Tell Them We Remember: The Story of the Holocaust
Susan D. Bachrach
ISBN: 978-0316074841

This text shares the facts of the Holocaust with students. It differs in its approach to the survivors; each survivor shares their likes, dislikes, hobbies, and interests independent of and before the Holocaust. Bachrach does an excellent job of painting a youthful and relevant face on an event that is often viewed as distant and in the past.

The Great Fire
Jim Murphy
ISBN: 978-0439203074

This informational text recounts the 1871 fire that destroyed much of Chicago. Murphy's text, created from primary sources, combines factual details with colorful word choices and suspense often reserved for fiction. The text includes multiple accounts that offer numerous viewpoints in one book. Sepia images, newspaper clippings, and photos are found on most pages.

The Making of America
Robert Johnston
ISBN: 9781709796114

This 200-page book is almost organized as an "anti-textbook." This text includes illustrations, photographs, and biographical data that chronicle important events in American history. The text can be used effectively with multiple informational text standards.

Young, Black, and Determined: A Biography of Lorraine Hansberry
Patricia McKissack and Frederick McKissack
ISBN: 978-0823413003

The McKissacks have a long history of crafting biographies that celebrate African-American and minority figures. With a blend of colorful language and important facts, the text presents the seldom-told story of Hansberry's contribution to the American canon and her struggles in life. This text offers numerous opportunities for students to connect ideas, events, and individuals while considering author's viewpoint and word choices.

CONTEMPORARY SUBJECTS

Chew On This: Everything You Don't Want to Know About Fast Food
Charles Wilson and Eric Schlosser
ISBN: 978-0618593941

This book explores the dangers of fast food and obesity. Humorous, yet disturbing at the same time, the text offers a high level of engagement while focusing on a serious topic. An adaptation of Schlosser's *Fast Food Nation*, this informational text offers a strong tone and point of view about the fast food industry.

71

The Teen's Guide to World Domination: Advice on Life, Liberty, and the Pursuit of Awesomeness

Josh Shipp

ISBN: 978-0312641542

Filled with wit and a dose of sarcasm, this book is an entertaining read. The word choices and clever analogies offer examples of organization and writer's craft. This text is one of the few examples where simple, teen-relevant content is presented in a fun way, but still offers the reader a great deal to examine in terms of style, message, voice, and organization. I would reserve this for my eighth graders, but it can be read by any grade level. Preview carefully for sensitive content and word choices.

The Ultimate Storm Survival Handbook

Warren Faidley

ISBN: 9781401602857

This handbook provides a wealth of facts about storms themselves, the damage they cause, and how to prepare in case of one. The text presents numerous claims with varying degrees of evidence to support the statements. Students are often engaged with the topic and eager to consider the suggestions and arguments put forth by Faidley.

Under Our Skin: Kids Talk about Race

Debbie Birdseye and Tom Birdseye

ISBN: 978-0823413256

Students share their perceptions of race in America. Told from the perspective of 12- and 13-year-olds, the text offers a candid peek into the multiplicity of experiences in America. Students have an opportunity to hear the voices of students their own age as they consider an issue often reserved for adults only.

What Do You Really Want? How to Set a Goal and Go for It! A Guide for Teens

Beverly K. Bachel

ISBN: 978-1575420851

This 130-page text is a how-to guide for preteens and teens. Reflective of the actual type of informational text reading that adults do, this selection is about self-improvement. Teens don't need prior knowledge or subject-area content to relate to the topic. I would recommend this book for the reluctant reader in your class. The student that typically asks (with a scowl): *"why are we reading this?"* when you present your classical favorites or historically-based texts will enjoy this book.

Word Play

"All my life I've looked at words as though I were seeing them for the first time."
Ernest Hemingway, author

Reading Informational Text Standard 4:
WORD PLAY

Sixth	Seventh	Eighth
Determine the meaning of words and phrases as they are used in a text, including figurative, connotative, and technical meanings.	Determine the meaning of words and phrases as they are used in a text, including figurative, connotative, and technical meanings; analyze the impact of a specific word choice on meaning and tone.	Determine the meaning of words and phrases as they are used in a text, including figurative, connotative, and technical meanings; analyze the impact of specific word choices on meaning and tone, including analogies or allusions to other texts.

GRADE LEVEL DIFFERENCES

The Word Play standard is very similar across grade levels. The standard for each grade level focuses on determining different types of meanings for words in context. Seventh- and eighth-grade students are asked to analyze the impact of those word choices. The only difference between the seventh- and eighth-grade standard is that the eighth-grade standard specifically mentions analogies and allusions. The skills remain exactly the same.

74

There are two different skills going on in the Word Play standard. The first deals with word meaning and the second deals with the impact of the word choice.

The first skill for each grade level focuses on determining the meaning of words. This means that students need to have some instruction in context clues and the practice of noting when they don't understand the meaning or the way that a word is used in a text.

The second skill set involved in the Word Play standard, just as the name implies, asks students to look at how words interact with the reader. When I think of this aspect of the Word Play standard, I visualize the reader being asked to dance, sing, run, hop, or skip with the text. How is that invitation extended? Does the text demand it? Does it quietly whisper the request? Is the request pensive? How do the words extend an invitation to the reader to engage with it? That is the essence of the Word Play standard.

This is not a study of vocabulary words in isolation or a dictionary exercise. This skill is about that invitation. How do the words engage the reader? Students are looking for how specific word choices set the tone or alter the meaning of the text.

This standard specifically asks students to consider three types of meanings: technical, connotative, and figurative. Focus on students recognizing that a word or phrase can be used to create different tones, take on multiple meanings, and help readers to experience the text differently through these choices.

Key Point

The reader is being asked to dance, sing, or skip with the text. *How is this invitation extended?* That is the essence of the Word Play standard.

1. Technical/Literal/Denotative

This type of word meaning is about understanding the actual definition of the word. A student could obviously just look up the word and figure out the definition, but these types of meanings may also rely on students recognizing the specialized meaning as it relates to the text content or area of study. For example, a *framer* may have multiple meanings depending on whether you are reading about home construction, art, or the constitution. The contextual meanings are still literal dictionary meanings, but students may need to be able to determine what is most appropriate based on the content and context of the piece.

2. Connotative

This type of meaning is the opposite of the denotative or technical meaning of a word. When students consider the connotative meaning, they are really considering different associations, feelings, and tones that those words evoke. An author's choice to use the words *very blunt* rather than *refreshingly candid* to describe a person is an illustrative example. Both sets of words could rightfully describe the same person, but each word choice establishes a very different connotative meaning.

3. Figurative

While technical and connotative are pretty straightforward, the definition of what counts as figurative can be exhaustive. Don't get bogged down in teaching every single literary device in an effort to classify it as a way to develop figurative meaning. Focus on figurative language as a counterpart to the connotative or literal definition of a word.

1 **Before students can analyze the word choices made within a text, they need to have a basis of where to start and what type of language could be used to help them verbalize what they think about those choices.** To lay this foundation, students need background knowledge about some of the terms used to describe word choices. Four key vocabulary words need to be used to introduce students to the Word Play standard: connotative, denotative, technical, and figurative.

2 **Introduce the words in pairs: connotative/ denotative, technical/figurative.** I like to introduce these in pairs because of the clear juxtaposition within each set. They help create a contrast and draw natural antonyms for students.

3 **Complete a Frayer model for one of the terms as a model for students.** The Frayer Model is a graphic organizer that is often used to study vocabulary and for word analysis. Students define the word used in their own words, and then identify relevant characteristics or facts associated with that word. Finally, students give examples and non-examples.

4 **Ask students to complete a Frayer model for each term, modeling and scaffolding as needed.** It is effective to complete the pairs on the same page or front and back.

5 **After students complete their Frayer Models, discuss what they found, exploring differences and similar perceptions of meaning.**

6 **After the class discussion, make one large Frayer Model for each word.** This can and should become an anchor chart for the Word Play standard.

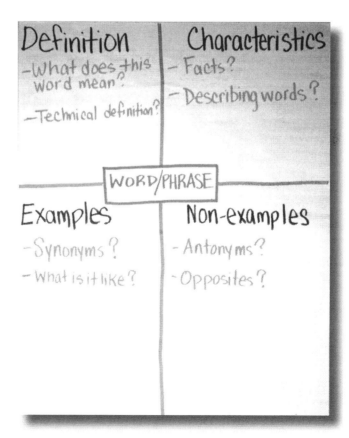

Definition
- What does this word mean?
- Technical definition?

Characteristics
- Facts?
- Describing words?

WORD/PHRASE

Examples
- Synonyms?
- What is it like?

Non-examples
- Antonyms?
- Opposites?

1 **Share with students that there are lots of ways to think about words.** *"Class, let me share a few ways that a reader can think about words."* Create an anchor chart (like the model here) with eight different ways to think about word choice.

2 **Select an informational text.** There are choices in the suggested titles list at the end of this chapter. Make copies for each student and project a large copy that you can write on. A document camera, interactive whiteboard, or overhead projector works well for this. *"As I read I am thinking about the words and what they mean. Keep in mind those different types of meanings that we discussed: connotative, denotative, technical, and figurative. More importantly, as a reader, I am constantly asking myself these questions on my chart. I am actively thinking about what is happening and what the different words may mean."*

3 **Make notes on the text and think out loud about your process.** Make authentic notes, focusing on word choice. Ask yourself questions and circle/highlight words that you are uncertain about. Explain that you are actively rereading and considering how the words make you feel, what the author may have intended for the words to make you think of, and what the tone is as you read.

4 **After you have read the text, go back and select two of the words or phrases within the text.** Ask the students to help you think about what these words mean. I like to share my thoughts about what I visualize, then ask students to share their own ideas, using the anchor chart as a point of reference. We go through the chart and really talk about the different types of questions that we can answer about these words. For the second word, invite students to select two or three of the questions from the anchor chart and respond to the questions about that word independently while you walk around and ask about their thinking.

5 **Come back together as a class and encourage a discussion about how they used the chart to think about the words.** Explain that they will try this same strategy when they read independently. Encourage them to use sticky notes to write and think about text if they are unable to write in the margins in the future.

Standard 4: Word Play
How do we think about words?

1. Visualization — What image do you have in your mind?
2. Tone/Mood — How does this word make you feel? Reader impact?
3. Opposites — What is it not? Antonyms? Non-examples?
4. In Context — How is it used? Context clues?
5. Associations — What is it like? Synonyms? Examples?
6. New Uses — How can you use this in your own writing?
7. Definitions — What is the technical, literal, or figurative meaning?
8. Writer's Choice — Why would the author use this word? What is the purpose or effect?

THE ORGANIZERS

Once you have explicitly introduced and modeled how to apply the strategies of the standard, now is the time to shift gears and provide students with multiple opportunities to practice the skill with their own reading in pairs, groups, and independently.

Students always need models, so each organizer has been completed based on *A Night to Remember* by Walter Lord. This text is suggested within the Common Core appendices as an appropriate informational text under the social studies strand. This particular text is used for each example under the Word Play standard for consistency and to offer the same book as a point of comparison for teachers.

1 Read (or reread) the first four pages of *A Night to Remember* with students. If you don't have a copy for each student, project the text so that all students can read it. Model how to complete the organizer using the samples that I have modeled next to each organizer or complete your own sample from the blank copy found in each section.

2 Once you model by explicitly completing the organizer yourself, your students will see the connection between the informational text and the organizer. You can provide blank copies of the organizer and allow students to select their own informational text, assign one from your class anthology, or select a title from the suggested book list within this chapter.

3 Students can complete the organizer when they read *any* informational text. This can be done as an assignment and can be repeated as many times as you want with any informational text that you choose. The sky is the limit! This allows for multiple opportunities to tailor the text to the student and maintain fidelity to the standard.

4 Once students have demonstrated mastery of the skill, don't stop using it. You want them to keep practicing. In the introduction of the book, I discussed the pitfalls of being a Checklist Teacher. Students need to keep perfecting their skill sets.

5 Reuse the same organizer, make it into an anchor chart, or post exemplars for students to reference later. You can add the organizer to a Word Play center, pair it with your school's reading incentive program to focus on Common Core skills with all reading activities, or use it daily as evidence of reading.

WORD PLAY WEB

This is really just a variation or adaptation of a Frayer model.

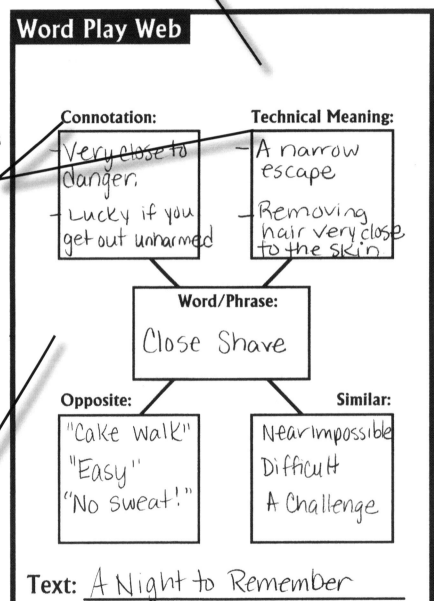

Word Play Web

Connotation:
- Very close to danger.
- Lucky if you get out unharmed

Technical Meaning:
- A narrow escape
- Removing hair very close to the skin

Word/Phrase:
Close Shave

Opposite:
"Cake Walk"
"Easy"
"No Sweat!"

Similar:
Near Impossible
Difficult
A Challenge

Text: A Night to Remember

Common Core
Buzzword

connotation & technical meanings show up across multiple grade levels in the common core standards.

Laminate multiple copies to use for a center with erasable markers.

Word Play Web

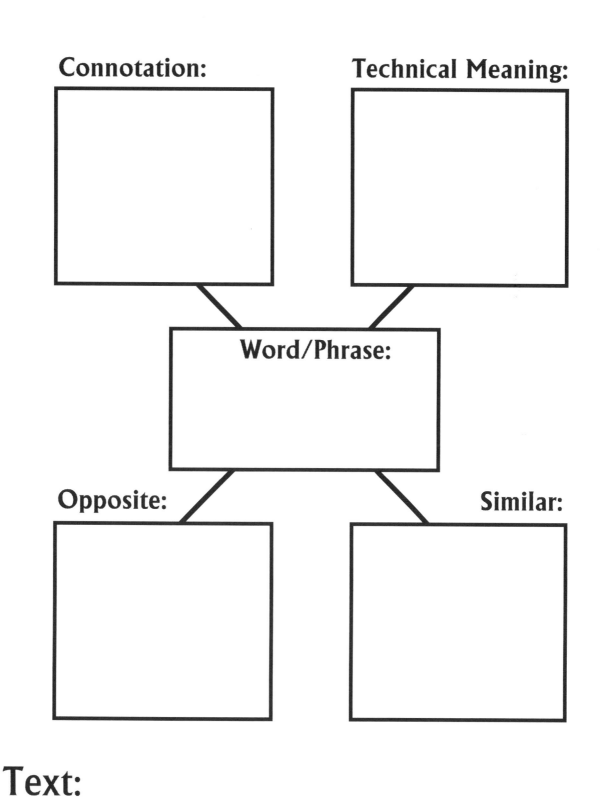

Connotation:

Technical Meaning:

Word/Phrase:

Opposite:

Similar:

Text: _____

©2013 The Common Core Guidebook. Intended for classroom use only. May not be reproduced or distributed without permission.

WHAT'S THE TONE?

Tone is challenging! For your students who really struggle, consider encouraging them just to think of how the author feels toward the topic. What feeling is communicated?

What's the Tone?

Pg. #	Word in Context	Tone	How does this impact the text?
1	High in the crow's nest of the New White Star Liner Titanic...	All knowing	This is figurative. It helps you get a picture in your head.
1	...the Titanic's maiden voyage	Sense of newness or freshness	It makes it seem very official compared to just saying 'the 1st voyage'.
3	The berg towered wet & glistened...	Imposing	Tower makes the iceberg seem insurmountable. The reader knows that it is, too.
3	They were dining saloon stewards, indulging in...	Selfish decadent	It creates an image of people who were just about themselves; carefree attitudes
3	It looked to the Fleet like a very close shave.	Suspenseful	Figurative The image of a man who could cut himself & get hurt or be totally okay. Creates suspense

Key Point

The focus is on how words are used in context, not in isolation.

Students can create a running tone log to record as they explore different informational text.

©2013 The Common Core Guidebook. Intended for classroom use only. May not be reproduced or distributed without permission.

What's the Tone?

Pg. #	Word in Context	Tone	How does this impact the text?

THINK LIKE AN AUTHOR!

This is an accessible organizer for even your more reluctant readers.

82

Think Like an Author!

Word/Phrase in Context:

This was the fifth night of the Titanic's maiden voyage.

Intended Effect:

This communicated that the Titanic was new & untested. This voyage was the first.

Opposite of:

Veteran
Experienced

Other Uses:

A maiden could just be a young girl. This would change it from an adjective to a noun.

Notice how few words are printed here. Students have to engage with word choices & craft their own ideas.

Alternatives for this box include:
- *a sentence of their own.*
- *a secondary use or meaning.*

©2013 The Common Core Guidebook. Intended for classroom use only. May not be reproduced or distributed without permission.

Think Like an Author!

Word/Phrase in Context:

Intended Effect:

Opposite of:

Other Uses:

DON'T BOX ME IN!

Let students determine how to use each box to show understanding of words in context.

84

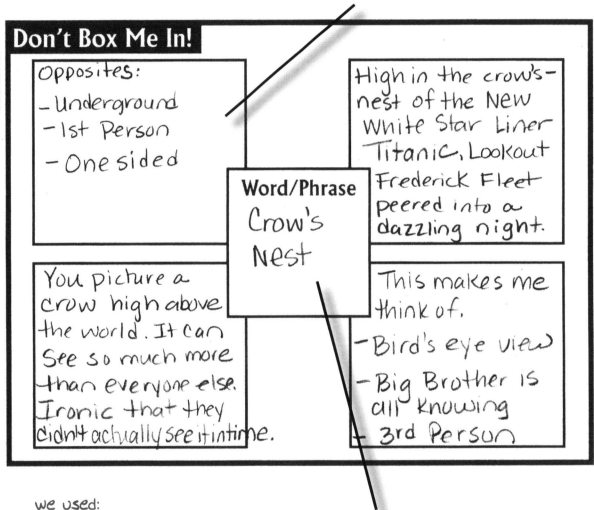

Don't Box Me In!

Opposites:
- Underground
- 1st Person
- One sided

High in the crow's-nest of the New White Star Liner Titanic, Lookout Frederick Fleet peered into a dazzling night.

Word/Phrase
Crow's Nest

You picture a crow high above the world. It can see so much more than everyone else. Ironic that they didn't actually see it in time.

This makes me think of.
- Bird's eye view
- Big Brother is all Knowing
- 3rd Person

we used:
- opposites
- word in context
- association
- visualization
for our four boxes.

This type of chart lets students be accountable for how they show their learning and understanding of word interactions.

©2013 The Common Core Guidebook. Intended for classroom use only. May not be reproduced or distributed without permission.

Don't Box Me In!

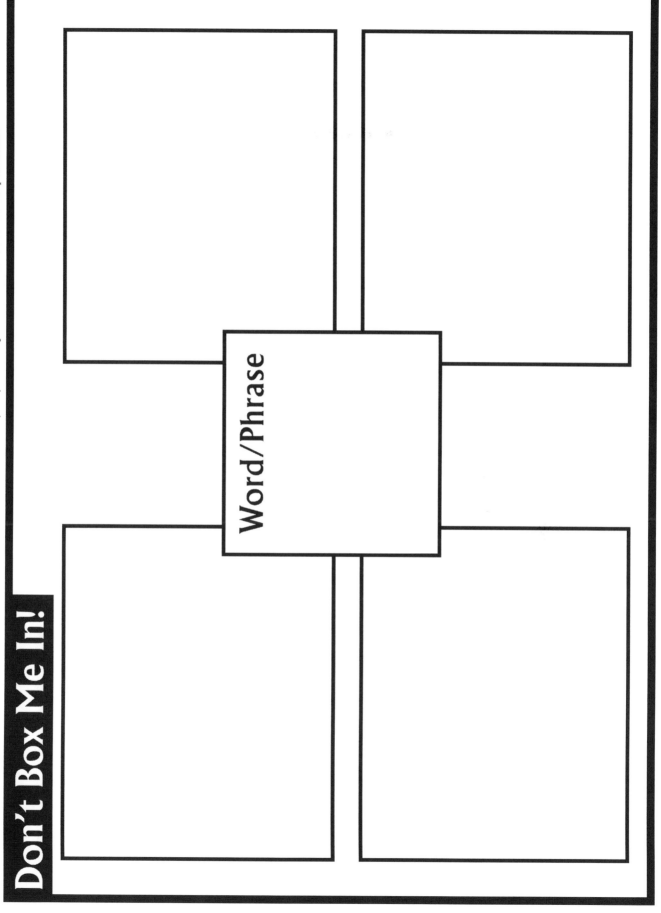

Word/Phrase

CHART THE MEANING

86

WARNING!

This can be overwhelming! An alternative is to focus on one at a time: connotative or technical.

Chart the Meaning

Word / Phrase	Sentence Found In:	Technical Meaning
maiden voyage	This was the 5th night of the Titanic's maiden voyage.	A maiden is a young, single girl. Voyage: trip

Connotative / Figurative Meaning

feeling of newness & the unknown.

Word / Phrase	Sentence Found In:	Technical Meaning
towered	The berg towered wet & glistened	To rise above or extend far upward.

Connotative / Figurative Meaning

Unstoppable & Huge (But we know it is not)

Irony!

Word / Phrase	Sentence Found In:	Technical Meaning
close Shave	It looked to the fleet like a very close Shave.	a narrow escape

Connotative / Figurative Meaning

Some that that was almost pretty bad.

Irony?

If you feel tempted to skip modeling—don't! Be sure to model all 3 examples. Students really struggle with the concept of thinking of words in so many different ways. Scaffolding is critical here.

Don't focus too much on grammar or language when students are jotting down their thoughts on the organizer. Stay focused on analysis & ideas about word choice.

Chart the Meaning

©2013 The Common Core Guidebook. Intended for classroom use only. May not be reproduced or distributed without permission.

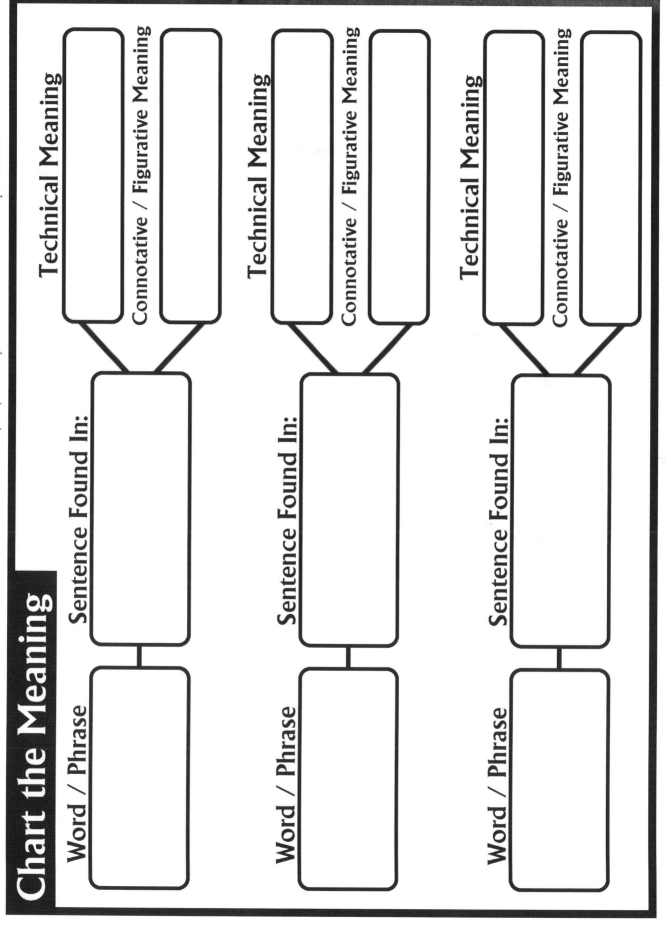

Technical Meaning

Connotative / Figurative Meaning

Sentence Found In:

Word / Phrase

Technical Meaning

Connotative / Figurative Meaning

Sentence Found In:

Word / Phrase

Technical Meaning

Connotative / Figurative Meaning

Sentence Found In:

Word / Phrase

ONLINE

Bottled Water is Silly — But So is Banning It
Charles Fishman
http://newswatch.nationalgeographic.com/2012/02/13/bottled-water-is-silly-but-so-is-banning-it/
This *National Geographic* article discusses bottled water use. The author presents a nuanced argument and is a bit tongue-in-cheek. The author's tone and his word choices are worth discussing. Students get to see an example of an informational text that also has a clear voice.

Picasso's Genius Revealed: He Used Common House Paint
Clara Moskowitz
http://www.livescience.com/26963-picasso-house-paint-x-rays.html
This news article makes the argument that Picasso did not use traditional artists' paint for his masterpieces. The text makes a claim and provides a wide variety of evidence to support the claim. This is a clear-cut and direct text that students can experiment with to analyze evidence.

CONTEMPORARY

Chew On This: Everything You Don't Want to Know About Fast Food
Charles Wilson and Eric Schlosser
ISBN: 978-0618593941
This book explores the dangers of fast food and obesity. Humorous, yet disturbing at the same time, the text offers a high level of engagement while focusing on a serious topic. An adaptation of Schlosser's *Fast Food Nation*, this informational text offers a strong tone and point of view about the fast food industry.

Geeks: How Two Lost Boys Rode the Internet out of Idaho
John Katz
ISBN: 978-0767906999
Katz, a journalist, details his correspondence with teen hackers, Jesse and Eric. As a self-proclaimed geek, Katz explores the complicated nature and evolution of geeks. Exploring issues of self-acceptance, transformation, and identity, this text offers connections for any middle school student. Creative word choices and accounts of both painful and gratifying experiences help craft an understanding of geekhood and the eventual "Geek Ascension" of each character.

The Digital Divide
Mark Bauerlein
ISBN: 978-1585428861

This is an excellent source for any teacher focusing on the evaluation of argument. Bauerlein's text includes essays written by a wide variety of authors. Each essay focuses on the relationship that the younger generation has to technology and digital communication. Each essay is organized by subtopics. Many of the pieces have been published before and offer great opportunities for analysis of author viewpoint, wordplay, perspectives, and supporting reasons. This is a particularly good choice for examining the evidence that each author provides to support specific claims.

The Teen's Guide to World Domination: Advice on Life, Liberty, and the Pursuit of Awesomeness
Josh Shipp
ISBN: 978-0312641542

Filled with wit and a dose of sarcasm, this book is an entertaining read. The word choices and clever analogies offer examples of organization and writer's craft. This text is one of the few examples where simple, teen-relevant content is presented in a fun way, but still offers the reader a great deal to examine in terms of style, message, voice, and organization. I would reserve this for my eighth graders, but it can be read by any grade level. Preview carefully for sensitive content and word choices.

Weird but True! Stupid Criminals: 100 Brainless Baddies Busted, Plus Wacky Facts
National Geographic
ISBN: 978-1426308611

This is a great choice for reluctant readers, as the content is light and a bit funny. The text provides examples of author's perspective and varying word choice allowing readers to determine the author's point of view toward the different subjects.

HISTORICAL

A Night to Remember
Walter Lord
ISBN: 978-0805077643

This text, suggested in the Common Core appendices, is classified as informational text. The book reads and is very much structured like a narrative account, so it will have a familiar feel for students. The events are retold based on interviews and firsthand sources. This text can easily be classified as historical fiction due to the narrative quality and creative liberties taken by the author. You will note that many of the Common Core informational text suggestions are historical fiction selections. Informational text is not just a synonym for nonfiction text. A teachable moment for this text is to explore the nuances associated with classifying books as solely one genre or the other.

A Young People's History of the United States: Columbus to the War on Terror
Howard Zinn and Rebecca Stefoff
ISBN: 978-1583228692

Zinn offers a perspective of American history that is rarely communicated by textbooks. He challenges many of the dominant narratives and accepted versions of historical events, making this a text that requires a critical eye and which is worthy of close analysis.

Shadow of the Titanic: The Extraordinary Stories of Those Who Survived
Andrew Wilson
ISBN: 978-1451671568

This text is based on the diaries, memories, letters, and interviews of the surviving members of the Titanic. Students can read specific chapters that follow individual survivors. The chapters chronicle how they remember that fateful day and how they coped after the event. Filled with colorful language, this text can be used in multiple ways to model the informational text standards.

Slavery Time When I Was Chillun
Belinda Hurmence
ISBN: 978-0399231940

While a full-length book, this text includes the accounts of twelve different African-Americans. The stories include childhood recollections based on interviews conducted in the 1930s, and each account can serve as a standalone text.

The Greatest: Muhammad Ali
Walter Dean Myers
ISBN: 978-0590543439

This book presents the life of Ali, but touches on the social issues that were prominent at the time. Segregation and racism are front and center in this text. Myers' language and comfortable writing style make it easy for students to tackle complex topics such as these. The writing also lends itself to analysis in terms of style, grammar, and punctuation. Appositives, dependent clauses, and various quotations make this an excellent mentor text for how writers use language and syntax to communicate as well.

They Stood Alone! 25 Men and Women Who Made a Difference
Sandra McLeod Humphrey
ISBN: 978-1616144852

The biographical vignettes chronicle the lives of numerous figures, including Margaret Mead, Henry David Thoreau, Nikola Tesla, and Neil Armstrong. This text can serve as a great reading introduction to the genre. These can be particularly powerful as exemplars for writing in the genre as well. Each piece provides a lesson in optimism, hard work, and courage in the face of adversity.

Author Memoirs

A Summer Life
Gary Soto
ISBN: 978-0440210245

This text is broken into three parts; each telling a different aspect of Soto's experiences. The chapters have quirky titles that show Soto's sly sense of humor: *The Chicks, The Shirt,* and *The Computer Date.* Soto uses humor to recount his youthful experiences in a way that builds an appreciation for nonfiction storytelling. Carefully preview each part for appropriate content for your students.

Knots in My Yo-Yo String
Jerry Spinelli
ISBN: 978-0679887911

Spinelli (*Crash, Loser,* and *Maniac Magee*) will be a familiar name to many middle school students. In this 160-page autobiography, he paints a picture of his life experiences with the same style he uses in his fiction books. Spinelli focuses on how he grew to become a writer. The conversational tone will hold the interest of most students and encourage your would-be future writers to hold tightly to their pens.

Travels with Charley in Search of America
John Steinbeck
ISBN: 978-0140053203

This 300-page travel diary is written in narrative style. Steinbeck and his dog, Charley, travel across America to explore the country. Steinbeck explains his motive for wanting to embark on this journey and presents a clear tone and point of view as he explores multiple towns and cities. The book has a wide variety of emotional moments. One challenge is that this text may seem disjointed to middle school students because it can seem more like a collection of disparate experiences, rather than a more linear memoir.

Essays and Letters

From Daughters to Mothers, I've Always Meant to Tell You: An Anthology of Letters
Constance Warloe
ISBN: 978-0671563257

In this 500-page informational text, over 75 women share letters that they have written to their mothers. Emotional and stirring, each letter addresses a variety of emotions, experiences, and situations. The voices are from notable and diverse poets, journalists, and cartoonists. They each have a flair for words, strong voices, and a commitment to telling their truth. The text can be treated as a whole, but it is probably most appropriate as a study of the individual letters or as a form of comparison among letters. This is most appropriate for older middle school and high school students. Preview for appropriateness.

Getups
Published within *Wouldn't Take Nothing for My Journey Now*
Maya Angelou
ISBN: 978-0553569070

Getups is an essay that explores multiple themes. This text encourages critical thinking about social, family, and identity issues. In this essay, Angelou explains how her son grew to be embarrassed of his mother's eccentric appearance when he was a child. She shares how he requested that she wear cardigans to school like the other mothers and even limit her visits. Angelou explores how she responded, the lessons she took away, and offers multiple points for readers to make inferences about.

The Best American Essays of the Century (The Best American Series)
Joyce Carol Oates and Robert Atwan
ISBN: 978-0618155873

These essays offer a wide range of topics and varying reading levels. This text offers multiple opportunities for shared and independent reading. The strength of this text is in the diversity of language, organization, and style. This one text could be used multiple times to model and teach all of the informational text standards.

The Best American Travel Writing 2012
Jason Wilson and William Vollman
ISBN: 978-0547808970

This text offers a collection of informational essays ranging from six or seven pages to over twenty-five. This should not be assigned as a set to simply read independently. The variety of language and higher-level vocabulary also makes the essays in this text a good choice for the Word Play standard. Close reading can easily be taught through these types of essays, offering multiple opportunities for shared reading, independent reading, and increasing text complexity among students. The strength of this text is in the diversity of language, organization, and style. This one text could be used multiple times to model and extend almost every informational text standard.

Text Structure

"It's not wise to violate the rules until you know how to observe them."
T. S. Eliot, poet

READING INFORMATIONAL TEXT STANDARD 5:
TEXT STRUCTURE

Sixth	Seventh	Eighth
Analyze how a particular sentence, paragraph, chapter, or section fits into the overall structure of a text and contributes to the development of the ideas.	Analyze the structure an author uses to organize a text, including how the major sections contribute to the whole and to the development of the ideas.	Analyze in detail the structure of a specific paragraph in a text, including the role of particular sentences in developing and refining a key concept.

GRADE LEVEL DIFFERENCES

Despite the variance in word choice, these standards are the same across each grade. Each grade level needs to analyze the text, by piece (sentence, section, paragraph, & chapter), and make sense of where that piece fits within the overall text. How does this help communicate the ideas of the bigger piece? What is the connection of the part to the whole? The eighth-grade language provides details and specificity to the description provided for sixth and seventh graders.

Informational text can be nonlinear. This means that it does not have to be read in the same way by everyone. Readers can "enter" the text in multiple ways. Think about a website. One reader might navigate the content very differently than another reader. The entry points are different. This standard demands that students recognize the different entry points and what function they serve. These entry points are the text structures. These structures can be physical or organizational. For students to arrive at mastery, they need to be able to:

▶ Recognize specific physical features of informational text.

▶ Identify specific organizational functions of informational text.

Sections within informational text are typically organized to function in one of the following ways:

1. Time Sequence

These sections of text are organized to sequentially unfold a series of events, steps, or ideas. This structure follows a chronological order.

2. Problem/Solution

Authors present a problem and offer a way to fix that problem.

3. Description

Authors explain a phenomena, event, idea, or person. This is often relegated to one section. Rarely is the overall purpose of a piece solely to describe.

4. Compare and Contrast

Authors explain how two or more things are alike or different. This type of structure lends itself to entire pieces, but also to sections of information that have a larger, different purpose. Look for call outs or images to depend on this structure as well.

5. Cause/Effect

Authors present causal relationships. These can extend to multiple subjects, ideas, and events. This is often tied to the Connections and Relationships standard.

It is important to note that a text could be structured primarily as a Problem/Solution piece, but there may be multiple components within that same text that serve *different* functions. For example, a recipe is a Time Sequence piece, but a photograph found within the recipe could be organized to function as a Cause/Effect piece, depending on what the photograph is. Students can also look for structural patterns in larger pieces or analyze one component such as a paragraph, sentence, or chapter of a text.

The standard specifically asks students to look at sentences, paragraphs, chapters, and sections. Sections can include parts that are often not classified as traditional text such as a Q&A, interviews, images, and multimedia components. Resist the urge to focus only on physical features such as bold print, titles, or headings. Those are specific to the elementary grade level standards and are introduced in first grade. The rigor should be on deconstructing higher level components and their specific functions.

1 **Ask students to think about the kind of jobs that they want to have when they grow up.** Call on student volunteers to share their career choices with the class.

2 **Explain that just like people have jobs, so do the parts of an informational text.** Each sentence, paragraph, image, or section plays a role in helping the readers understand the text. *"Well, since you guys have shared a bit about the role you want to take on in the future, let me talk about how that relates to reading informational text. Each part has a role or job. There are no coincidences or sections just there for no reason at all. Each piece has a job, a role, a structure, and a function."*

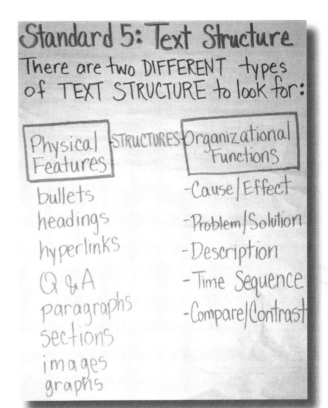

3 **Create a chart, like the one pictured here, that displays the different roles that informational text sections can have.** Many people refer to these as *organizational structures*. I like to think of *structures* as the umbrella term. These can include physical features *and* organizational functions. Students can rely on this anchor chart throughout the year when analyzing text.

4 **Introduce models of each structure.** You want to use short paragraphs or text excerpts to do this. A great strategy is to use a science or social studies text or a basal reader. Each of these structures can easily be found in short, easy formats. I select a few textbooks and place a sticky note during my planning on the places where I notice specific structures, then photocopy or provide the text for the students to read as we study each one.

Extend the
Thinking

Instructional Variations:

▶ Introduce one structure at a time, slowly introducing more throughout the year to match your text choices and curriculum needs.

▶ Introduce on or two at a time that fit well with your fellow content area teachers. What type of reading is coming up in science? What types of informational text will students need in social studies?

95

TEXT STRUCTURE **THINK-ALOUD**

1 Research Based

Select examples of informational text that match each of the different structures you introduced earlier. I find that it is easiest to pull these from online news sources or photocopy a page from an anthology that shows the structure. Another quick and accurate source is a science or social studies book. These texts are rich with graphics and multiple entry points for the reader. It is easy to do a visual scan and select an excerpt that is organized in multiple ways. For this lesson it is not important just yet that students identify different organizational structures within a larger text. You are still helping them to conceptualize the structures, so a small excerpt is appropriate.

"Structural elements in expository texts vary; therefore, it is important to introduce students to the components of various texts throughout the school year. It is also important to teach and model the use of these components properly at the beginning of the school year. The recognition and use of text organization are essential processes underlying comprehension and retention."

(Akhondi, et al., 2011, p. 369)

2 **Read each of your selected text excerpts aloud with the students.** After you read each one, discuss what type of structure you noted. What function did it serve? How does it work? Ask students to engage with you as you try to encourage a discussion about each excerpt. Make sure that you classify each of the excerpts to the corresponding text structure and function.

3 **Using the initial anchor chart, add the signal words as well or create individual signal word charts that show words to look for.** Students should create their own charts as you introduce and model each feature. This can be ongoing throughout the year or taught as a longer unit that introduces each structure.

Structure	Purpose	Signal Words
Time Sequence	Chronological explanation, steps, order, series	first, next, then, finally, following
Problem & Solution	Concerns or problems that need to be solved	problems, concerns, issues, solve, confusion
Description	describe an event, idea, or person	for example, about, characteristics, traits, definition, meaning
Compare & Contrast	show differences and/or similarities	By comparison, unlike, opposite, on the other hand, differences, similarities
Cause & Effect	Show the relationship between two causal events, individuals, ideas or actions.	if...then, impact, because, as a result, caused, parallels, effect

My Anchor Chart is organized by the organizational function (structure) matched to the signal words.

THE ORGANIZERS

Once you have explicitly introduced and modeled how to apply the strategies of the standard, now is the time to shift gears and provide students with multiple opportunities to practice the skill with their own reading in pairs, groups, and independently.

Students always need models, so each organizer has been completed based on the online news article: *Five Reasons Not to Drink Bottled Water* by Chris Baskind. This free news article is listed in the suggested text section and can be accessed at: http://www.mnn.com/food/healthy-eating/stories/5-reasons-not-to-drink-bottled-water. This particular text is used for each example under the Text Structure standard for consistency and to offer the same text as a point of comparison for teachers.

1 Read (or reread) the entire news article with students. If you don't have a copy for each student, project the text so that all students can read it. Model how to complete the organizer with the sample provided here or complete your own sample using one of the blank copies.

2 Once you model by explicitly completing the organizer yourself, your students will see the connection between the informational text and the organizer. You can provide blank copies of the organizer and allow students to select their own informational text, assign one from your class anthology, or select a title from the suggested book list within this chapter.

3 Students can complete the organizer when they read *any* informational text. This can be done as an assignment and can be repeated as many times as you want with any informational text that you choose. The sky is the limit! This allows for multiple opportunities to tailor the text to the student and maintain fidelity to the standard.

4 Once students have demonstrated mastery of the skill, don't stop using it. You want them to keep practicing. In the introduction of the book, I discussed the pitfalls of being a Checklist Teacher. Students need to keep perfecting their skill sets.

5 Reuse the same organizer, make it into an anchor chart, or post exemplars for students to reference later. You can add the organizer to a center, pair it with your school's reading incentive program to focus on Common Core skills with all reading activities, or use it daily as evidence of reading.

FEATURE CHART

Writing
Connection

This can also be connected to student writing. Understanding the function helps students use the feature or pattern effectively in their own writing.

Feature Chart

Central Idea: Bottled Water causes problems!

Text Feature	Function	How does this make the text easier to understand?
Problems are all numbered and in bold.	Lists Problems	Easy to find and review quickly
Heading & ¶: "What Can You do?"	Solution	Q+A makes it seem easy
Hyperlinks at the end.	Description	More information, but reader is in control of it.
Paragraphs for reason 3 + 4	Cause & Effect	Makes the impact (effect) easy to understand.

I love the combination of the feature & function here. Don't separate the two—they work well in conjunction.

Be sure to keep an anchor chart up with examples & definitions of each type of organizational function.

©2013 The Common Core Guidebook. Intended for classroom use only. May not be reproduced or distributed without permission.

Feature Chart

Central Idea:

Text Feature	Function	How does this make the text easier to understand?

PART TO WHOLE

This is a great organizer for students to work on collaboratively, dividing up the tasks & comparing notes about their choices.

Symbols and shorthand are okay for this type of textual analysis.

Part to Whole	5 Reasons Not to Drink Bottled Water By: Chris Baskind		
Sentence	**Paragraph**	**Section**	**Other**
Text #2 "On the other hand, water systems in the developed world..."	Paragraph under #3	All of the bold, numbered sections	Final ¶: What Can You Do?
Function Compare & Contrast US and world wide water systems. Tap water vs. bottled water regulations.	Cause & Effect to show readers the effect of the waste caused by bottled water.	Lists all of the problems with bottled water.	This is a solution for all of the problems in the article.

Common Core **Buzzword**

The standard relies on the sentence, paragraph & section terminology. This is the language from the common core standards. Refer to these with fidelity.

©2013 The Common Core Guidebook. Intended for classroom use only. May not be reproduced or distributed without permission.

Part to Whole

	Sentence	Paragraph	Section	Other
Text				
Function				

WHAT'S YOUR FUNCTION?

After using this organizer often, students should be able to complete this for every informational text that they read as a form of structural analysis. Pair this with other comprehension quizzes or tasks to provide evidence of Standard 5 with each reading.

What's Your Function?	Text: Chris Baskind
Feature	**Function**
Bold, Numbered list (5 of them)	Lists the problems w/ bottled water
Final paragraph: What Can You Do?	A solution to the problem
Paragraph for reason #2	Compare & Contrast water regulation systems
Paragraph for reason #3	Cause & Effect to show problems caused by waste.
Paragraph for reason #4	Cause & Effect of low consumer concern.
Introduction	Description of bottled water industry + marketing.
Paragraph for reason #1	Compare & Contrast (shows $$ differences)

Notice my spelling error. I left it & we talked about it later. Reinforce that students don't need to be perfect. Many students use an error as a reason to get distracted and start over. Focus on the task! Surface errors come second.

💡 Extend the
Thinking

These types of lists can go on forever! Post these in a center or maintain a class list of how students notice features and functions in their informational text selections.

What's Your Function?

©2013 The Common Core Guidebook. Intended for classroom use only. May not be reproduced or distributed without permission.

Text: _____

Feature	Function

African-Americans in the Old West
Tim McGowen
ISBN: 978-0516263489
This text is a lower-level reader; all students should be able to access the text easily. The lack of challenge to understand the content allows students ample time to consider the organization, structure, and text features within the book. The text follows historical timelines and introduces students to concepts and ideas that they are probably unfamiliar with. The text is an excellent match for the Text Structure standard.

Before Columbus: The Americas of 1491
Charles C. Mann
ISBN: 978-1416949008
This informational text, organized similar to a photo-essay text, provides beautiful images that document the pre-Columbian animals and people. The text is definitely an easy read for middle school students and offers an entry point for readers of any level. Students get a quick snapshot of multiple text features (captions, call outs, images, photos, and diagrams). When using this text, focus on why a text feature is useful. What information does it relay? What organizational pattern does it follow? What question does it answer? This text has the potential to engage students in an introductory conversation about a variety of structures and the ease of reading.

Days of Jubilee: The End of Slavery in the United States
Patricia McKissack and Frederick McKissack
ISBN: 978-0590107648
While the signing of the Emancipation Proclamation is historically referred to as the end of slavery, sadly, it was not. Many slaves waited years for their freedom. This hopeful day became known as the Day of Jubilee. Multiple perspectives are included based on first-hand source documents. This is an excellent match for social studies units that explore the Civil War or The Civil Rights Movement. This text offers a wide variety of organizational structures. Students can examine sections to determine if they are organized to describe, sequence, or compare and contrast ideas, events, or individuals. This text is historically accurate, yet accessible for all readers.

Freedom Walkers: The Story of the Montgomery Bus Boycott
Russell Freedman
ISBN: 978-0823421954
This text combines personal recollections and historical accounts of the Montgomery Bus Boycott. Legendary civil rights activists such as Parks, King, and Colvin are included in a photo-essay format.

Geeks: How Two Lost Boys Rode the Internet out of Idaho
John Katz
ISBN: 978-0767906999
Katz, a journalist, details his correspondence with teen hackers, Jesse and Eric. As a self-proclaimed geek, Katz explores the complicated nature and evolution of geeks. Exploring issues of self-acceptance, transformation, and identity, this text offers connections for any middle school student. Creative word choices and accounts of painful and gratifying experiences help craft an understanding of geekhood and the eventual "Geek Ascension" of each character.

Healthy Diet: End the Guesswork with These Nutrition Guidelines
Mayo Clinic Staff
http://www.mayoclinic.com/health/healthy-diet/NU00200
This article is an excellent piece to use when exploring how online articles are structured. At first glance, the article appears to be only a few paragraphs long. Students have to navigate through the hyperlinks on the left to move through the headings, organized by central ideas, with various organizing structures within each section. This is a solid example of how online informational text can be structured.

How the States Got Their Shapes
Mark Stein
ISBN: 978-0061431395
Stein's 350-page book, divided by state, presents facts and images to explain why states are shaped the way that they are. Some parts are written in narrative style, while others rely more on archival evidence to explain the rationale behind the various shapes. The text is easy to read and can be approached by state. Students can easily compare and contrast the shape origins between different states, or use the state chapters to supplement more targeted units of study across the curriculum.

Scholastic Science World
www.scholastic.com/scienceworld
Science World includes short, easy articles that are often rich with data, facts, statistics, and a great deal of support. Students can read this magazine to locate textual evidence, analyze reasoning and the strength of an argument. Similar to most of the other *Scholastic* publications, the content is engaging and diverse.

The Great Homework Debate: Is Homework Helpful or Harmful to Students?
Cory Ames
http://www.scilearn.com/blog/homework-debate-is-homework-helpful-or-harmful.php
This article looks at homework from a neutral position. The author evaluates the purpose and structure of homework assignments in school. Hyperlinks and references to sources are included, making this is an excellent informational text to examine for evidence.

The Making of America
Robert Johnston
ISBN: 9781709796114
This 200-page book is almost organized as an "anti-textbook." This text includes illustrations, photographs, and biographical data that chronicle important events in American history. The text can be used effectively with multiple informational text standards.

What is Fracking?
http://www.energyfromshale.org/hydraulic-fracturing/what-is-fracking?
This article presents an argument for fracking. Students are presented with reasons why this practice is a critical component of America's future energy plan. Using images and text, the article presents information and details to support the expansion and use of fracking as a national effort.

Author's Point of View

"The most fatal illusion is the settled point of view."
Brooks Atkinson, *New York Times* reviewer

READING INFORMATIONAL TEXT STANDARD 6:
AUTHOR'S POINT OF VIEW

Sixth	Seventh	Eighth
Determine an author's point of view or purpose in a text and explain how it is conveyed in the text.	Determine an author's point of view or purpose in a text and analyze how the author distinguishes his or her position from that of others.	Determine an author's point of view or purpose in a text and analyze how the author acknowledges and responds to conflicting evidence or viewpoints.

GRADE LEVEL DIFFERENCES

In sixth grade, students are expected to determine the author's purpose or viewpoint and show specifically how the text is developed to communicate this. In seventh and eighth grade, students are expected to move beyond simple identification of point of view and its development. The standard demands that students evaluate how the author addresses counterclaims and opposing viewpoints.

108

There are two common misconceptions about this standard. One misconception is that students only need to identify the author's purpose in terms of genre. This is an unfortunate misread. This confusion leads teachers to teach lessons that focus on distinguishing between entertaining, informing, or persuading. Students try to classify text neatly into one category when this approach is used. Think about most informational writing. By its very definition, the purpose is to inform readers. The format could be entertaining in nature, contain persuasive elements, or simply rely on a variety of elements. Sticking to this formulaic instruction of author's point of view is much too limiting.

The second misconception is that point of view focuses on narration style. This leads to lessons on first, second, and third person. While valuable, the focus of this standard is not on narration type. If the instructional focus stays on classification of narration style, students will miss the entire core of the standard.

This standard is about what the author is trying to say. What is the author's purpose? Why is he saying this? What is her position? On a higher level, students are effectively asking how the text is attempting to position them. What assumptions does the author make? How are counterarguments considered? Analysis should be centered on the author and his or her views and stances. A useful concept to consider when teaching this is that everything is an argument. When authors write about butterflies, it is never simply to spread facts. What are they arguing? Is it that butterflies are valuable and deserve to be appreciated?

To teach this standard, particularly in the upper grades, you must be intentional with your early text selections. In order for students to analyze how an author responds to conflicting evidence and viewpoints (8th grade) or distinguish his or her position from that of others (7th grade), the text choices need to make an identifiable argument and have some opposition. The suggested text list at the end of this chapter is organized to provide examples that present clear arguments. This standard also offers great possibilities for integration into writing instruction. Students working on argument papers can easily share their work with each other and analyze the different viewpoints. This provides peer review time and opportunities for feedback.

The central focus of this standard is looking at the composition of a piece of informational text in order to determine:

1. What is the author's perspective?

2. How did the author develop or explain his perspective?

3. How does the author respond to opposing or conflicting information?

Extend the Thinking

Examining perspective can lead to multiple critical literacy opportunities. Encourage students to critique and look for what voices are missing or marginalized in text. What assumptions does the text make?

1 **Write *Point of View* on the board.** Ask students what they think the term means. Have a discussion and let students talk it through.

2 **Introduce the skill for this standard.** *"We are going to talk about point of view today. I won't ask you about your point of view, but we are going to think about how to determine an author's point of view when we read his or her work."*

3 **Create an anchor chart with the students or have them create one of their own in a location that they can reference.** *"There are a few questions that will help you think about the author's point of view. We are going to record them here, so that you can refer to them as we talk more about point of view."*

4 **Emphasize that these questions all ask the same thing, but use different words.** They are just there to help students think about the author and his or her views as they read a text.

5 **Read an informational text aloud from the suggested list or your own selection.** I like to use a short informational picture book, website excerpt, movie review, letter to the editor, or news article that can be easily read and understood for this level of the introduction. *"I am going to share an informational text with you. As I read this aloud, I would like for you to ask yourself the questions listed on our anchor chart to see if you can come up with an answer. Just like everything we practice, be prepared to provide some evidence to support what you think."*

6 **After you read the text, challenge students to answer one of the questions from the anchor chart about that text.** When they answer, specifically ask them to point out evidence from the text that helped them infer the point of view.

7 **Ask students to summarize what they learned about today.** *"The next time we will do exactly what we did today, but we will write a bit about the very things we talked about today. Can I have a volunteer to tell me what we learned today?"*

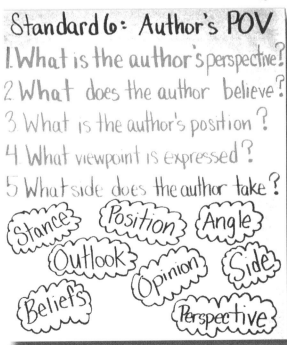

Standard 6: Author's POV
1. What is the author's perspective?
2. What does the author believe?
3. What is the author's position?
4. What viewpoint is expressed?
5. What side does the author take?

Stance · Position · Angle · Outlook · Opinion · Side · Beliefs · Perspective

1 **Read one of the short One-Minute Reviews found at rogerebert.com, or another source, out loud.** As you read, remember to think out loud, sharing questions or thoughts so that students can have access to the inner dialogue you have as you read. *"I am going to share a text with you where an author has written a short informational text paragraph that describes a movie. The author has an obvious point of view expressed in his writing. As we read together, I want you to think about the questions from our Point of View anchor chart (from the introduction lesson) and mentally answer them. As you form your response, look for proof in the movie review. How do you know? What actual words help you determine the author's point of view? Tone? Attitudes toward the film?"*

Research Based

"A major goal of the guided instruction phase in the gradual release of responsibility model is to create an environment for students where they can begin to apply what they are learning. Mastery is not the goal. The teacher is there to provide scaffolds to support and guide learners."

(Frey & Fisher, 2010, p. 85).

110

2 **When you finish, complete a quick sentence frame (see the anchor chart example on this page) to describe the author's point of view.** Ask students to help you find clues in the text that support your decision about the author's point of view. Repeat with two to four more movie reviews.

3 **Select a new text that is slightly longer and read together.** For seventh- and eighth-grade students it is important to select a piece that acknowledges a counterargument. Discuss this with students and consider the word choice and clues as well. *"This is the process we will follow when we think about the author's point of view. Let's try that with a longer piece of text now."*

4 **Repeat this activity as needed based on your observations of your students.** Release responsibility and encourage them to try this in pairs or individually.

Standard 6: Author's POV
Sentence Frames
Based on the text, this author believes _____.
Evidence of this opinion include _____.

After reading this text, I noticed _____. This helped me understand the author's view of _____. Other examples of this viewpoint include _____.

THE ORGANIZERS

Once you have explicitly introduced and modeled how to apply the strategies of the standard, now is the time to shift gears and provide students with multiple opportunities to practice the skill with their own reading in pairs, groups, and independently.

Students always need models, so each organizer has been completed based on *Geeks* by John Katz. This text is suggested within the Common Core appendices as an appropriate informational text under the reading strand. If you used the introduction from *Geeks* before with the Central Ideas standard or the Connections & Relationships standard, this will be very simple to model. Refer back to what you read in the introduction of the book and talk about the content. Students can now easily focus on how the organizers work. This particular text is used for each example under the Author's Point of View standard for consistency and to offer the same book as a point of comparison for teachers.

1 Read (or reread) the introduction from *Geeks* with students. If you don't have a copy for each student, project the text so that all students can read it. Model how to complete the organizer using the samples that I have modeled next to each organizer or complete your own sample from the blank copy found in each section.

2 Once you model by explicitly completing the organizer yourself, your students will see the connection between the informational text and the organizer. You can provide blank copies of the organizer and allow students to select their own informational text, assign one from your class anthology, or select a title from the suggested book list within this chapter.

3 Students can complete the organizer when they read *any* informational text. This can be done as an assignment and can be repeated as many times as you want with any informational text that you choose. The sky is the limit! This allows for multiple opportunities to tailor the text to the student and maintain fidelity to the standard.

4 Once students have demonstrated mastery of the skill, don't stop using it. You want them to keep practicing. In the introduction of the book, I discussed the pitfalls of being a Checklist Teacher. Students need to keep perfecting their skill sets.

5 Reuse the same organizer, make it into an anchor chart, or post exemplars for students to reference later. You can add the organizer to a Point of View center, pair it with your school's reading incentive program to focus on Common Core skills with all reading activities, or use it daily as evidence of reading.

POINT OF VIEW CLUES

Add in-text citations here if your school teaches those in 6-8.

Great anchor chart for any text. Enlarge on a poster maker and laminate.

Point of View Clues

What the text says:

Where does it begin, this sense of being The Other? It can come early on, when you find yourself alone in your childhood bedroom... playing by yourself. Or in middle school, when the jocks turn on you.

Clues

"Alone"
"By Yourself"
Lots of reference to being on your own.

Clues

"The Other"
Proper noun makes it seem like a formal place or title.

Clues

"Jocks turn on you."
Popular v. Not popular ?

Author's Point of View:

People labeled as geeks have to deal with alienation & lots of challenges about acceptance.

Encourage students to use ? when they are unsure, have additional questions, or are talking back to the text.

112

©2013 The Common Core Guidebook. Intended for classroom use only. May not be reproduced or distributed without permission.

Point of View Clues

What the text says:

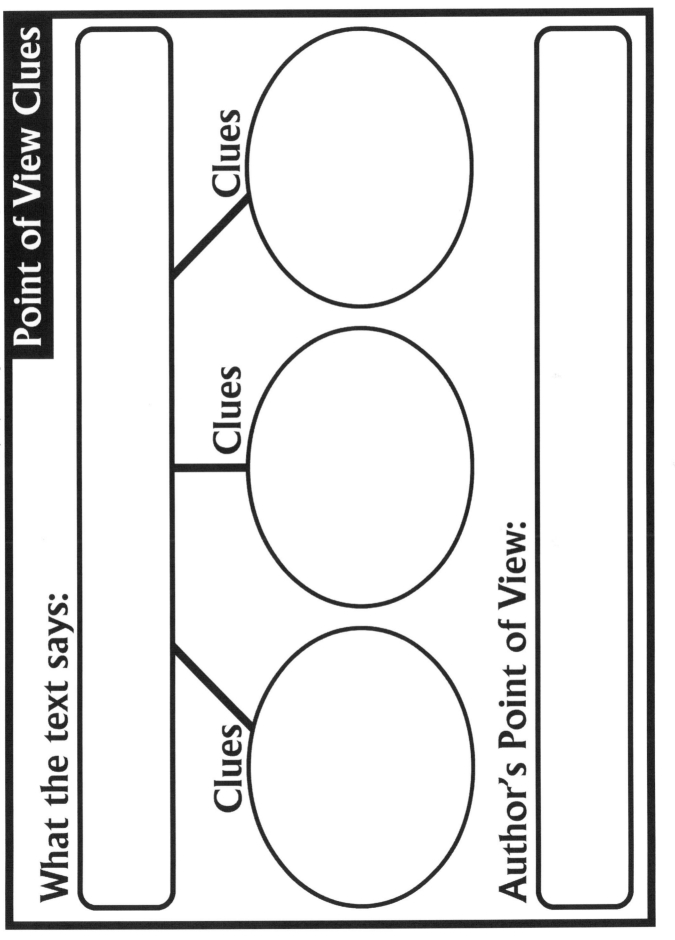

Clues

Clues

Clues

Author's Point of View:

POV EXPLANATION

When I model this organizer, I stick to the introduction of *Geeks* because the entire text is much too long for a think-aloud. Remember that you want the text that you model to be accessible and able to be explored in detail for your modeling.

114

Page / Section	Excerpt / Passage	Author's Point of View with Explanation
xxiii	I wrote several additional Hotwired columns about geekhood, and emails poured in by the metric ton.	The geek audience is huge. Many people wanted to identify with Katz's experiences.
xxii	We are the only irreplaceable people in the building. Welcome to the geek kingdom.	Geeks cannot be replaced because they are so talented. ?BIG assumption!
xviii	...at some point somewhere you brush against the outsiderness-among geeks, it's the one common rite of passage.	All geeks are outsiders in some way.
xvii	The alienation is sometimes mild, sometimes savage.	Alienation is tough and overwhelming. *Pretty bad → Savage*

POV Explanation

A handmade example of this could be a simple T-chart with the excerpt and POV on opposing sides.

Reinforce that students are really always working on Standard One: Textual Evidence. This is the umbrella standard for all of the other standards.

©2013 The Common Core Guidebook. Intended for classroom use only. May not be reproduced or distributed without permission.

POV Explanation

Page / Section	Excerpt / Passage	Author's Point of View with Explanation

POINT OF VIEW CHART

Ideas can be general or complete sentences.

Writing Connection

This can become a good idea organizer for a paper on the three main points within an informational text.

Topic/Ideas	Author's Point of View	My Point of View
Middle + High School Experiences	Geek are isolated and do not have many friends. ✻ Being a geek is lonely	I don't think this is true for Kids today. Geek culture is almost ✻ like a fad. Kind of cool.
Value of 'Geeks'	Geeks are in high demand by colleges & businesses.	I think this is a stereotype. If you have tech skills you aren't automatically a geek. All geeks are not tech geniuses.
Acceptance	Geeks have a secret society & they are everywhere. 'Accidental Empires'	Just like in high school or middle school, being a geek is okay. I agree.

Point of View Chart

Often students will craft their own POV statements that are simply responses to the authors' POV. That is very appropriate.

116

©2013 The Common Core Guidebook. Intended for classroom use only. May not be reproduced or distributed without permission.

Topic/Ideas	Author's Point of View	My Point of View

Point of View Chart

FOUR SQUARE POINT OF VIEW

I show students how to use ellipses here. The point is not to fill the page with lots of text. The point is to locate meaningful textual evidence to explain POV.

118

POV: Caltech, Stanford & MIT are safe places for
Proof: "geeks"

"Elite geek incubators like Caltech, Stanford & MIT..."

POV: No one can box in a geek or define them in
Proof: one way.

"What, exactly is a geek? After years of trying to grapple with this question, I still find it largely unanswerable."

Topic: Struggles being a "geek"

POV: Geeks are alienated.

Proof:

"Where does it begin, this sense of being the Other?"

POV: Alienation is very hard to deal with.

Proof:

"The alienation is sometimes mild, sometimes savage."

Four Square POV

Proofs = Textual Evidence

Key Point

Similar to the central Ideas standard, there can be multiple POVs within one text. Focus on the proofs.

©2013 The Common Core Guidebook. Intended for classroom use only. May not be reproduced or distributed without permission.

Four Square POV

POV:

Proof:

POV:

Proof:

Topic:

POV:

Proof:

POV:

Proof:

This standard works well with biographies, historical accounts, or first-person accounts of experiences and events. Each selection here offers a clear perspective on a subject or set of experiences.

ANTHOLOGIES/ MULTIPLE ACCOUNTS

Now is Your Time! The African-American Struggle for Freedom
Walter Dean Myers
ISBN: 978-0064461207

This collection of biographical vignettes is riveting and thought provoking. Short, yet powerful in content, each explores the life and struggle of a different African-American. Students will learn as much from the content as they do about analysis. This book pairs well with thematic units of courage and determination.

Something to Declare
Julia Alvarez
ISBN: 978-0452280670

This essay anthology explores the experiences of Julia Alvarez. The essays all explore a different topic, but focus on the concepts of identity formation, self-esteem, the American Dream, and culture. Alvarez's own multiple conceptions of identity as an American, Dominican, parent, and writer are explored throughout the text. Several particular essays of note within the anthology include: *Grandfather's Blessings, Our Papers, I Want to be Miss America* and *My English*. This text touches on topics that all students can relate to.

They Stood Alone! 25 Men and Women Who Made a Difference
Sandra McLeod Humphrey
ISBN: 978-1616144852

The biographical vignettes chronicle the lives of numerous figures, including Margaret Mead, Henry David Thoreau, Nikola Tesla, and Neil Armstrong. This text can serve as a great reading introduction to the genre. These can be particularly powerful as exemplars for writing in the genre as well. Each piece provides a lesson in optimism, hard work, and courage in the face of adversity.

HISTORICAL

A Young People's History of the United States: Columbus to the War on Terror
Howard Zinn and Rebecca Stefoff
ISBN: 978-1583228692

Zinn offers a perspective of American history that is rarely communicated by textbooks. He challenges many of the dominant narratives and accepted versions of historical events, making this a text that requires a critical eye and which is worthy of close analysis.

Chasing Lincoln's Killer
James Swanson
ISBN: 978-0545204705

This text reads like a mystery or thriller. The 12-day manhunt for John Wilkes Booth is recounted through trial manuscripts, archival data, and interviews. The text offers numerous historical connections and a wealth of examples to explore point of view and word play.

Days of Jubilee: The End of Slavery in the United States
Patricia McKissack and Frederick McKissack
ISBN: 978-0590107648

While the signing of the Emancipation Proclamation is historically referred to as the end of slavery, sadly, it was not. Many slaves waited years for their freedom. This hopeful day became known as the Day of Jubilee. Multiple perspectives are included based on first-hand source documents. This is an excellent match for social studies units that explore the Civil War or The Civil Rights Movement. This text offers a wide variety of organizational structures. Students can examine sections to determine if they are organized to describe, sequence, or compare and contrast ideas, events, or individuals. This text is historically accurate, yet accessible for all readers.

Dear Miss Breed: True Stories of the Japanese American Incarceration During World War II and a Librarian Who Made a Difference
Joanne Oppenheim
ISBN: 978-0439569927

Dear Miss Breed is a stirring account of World War II injustices. The text follows the experiences of a group of Japanese-Americans who were interned during the war in 1942. The text unfolds through a series of letters sent to San Diego librarian Clara Breed, archival materials, and interviews with the letters' grown-up authors. Oppenheim encourages readers to interrogate primary sources and critically examine documents from this era on their own. The author positions herself as an advocate for critical analysis and actively challenging the dominant narrative presented about World War II.

Four Perfect Pebbles: A Holocaust Story
Lila Perl
ISBN: 978-0380731886

This text traces the experiences of Marion Blumenthal and her family as they experience the horrors of the Holocaust. While the events are expectably mature, the writing is appropriate for middle school readers. The personal narrative format offers a familiar style for students to understand. The book does not have the intensity of *Night* or *The Cage*, but the depth of information is profound and expansive.

The Great Fire
Jim Murphy
ISBN: 978-0439203074

This informational text recounts the 1871 fire that destroyed much of Chicago. Murphy's text, created from primary sources, combines factual details with colorful word choices and suspense often reserved for fiction. The text includes multiple accounts that offer numerous viewpoints in one book. Sepia images, newspaper clippings, and photos are found on most pages.

Tell Them We Remember: The Story of the Holocaust
Susan D. Bachrach
ISBN: 978-0316074841

This text shares the facts of the Holocaust with students. It differs in its approach to the survivors; each survivor shares their likes, dislikes, hobbies, and interests independent of and before the Holocaust. Bachrach does an excellent job of painting a youthful and relevant face on an event that is often viewed as distant and in the past.

Warriors Don't Cry: A Searing Memoir of the Battle to Integrate Little Rock's Central High
Melba Pattillo Beals
ISBN: 978-1416948827

This is the abridged version of a text commonly read by high school and even college students. 100 pages shorter, this text is manageable for your older middle school students. The text is well-organized and provides a great deal of background information on the desegregation of Little Rock High School. Up close and personal experiences with being kicked, hit, and spit-upon are chronicled to paint a vivid picture of the injustices of this era. This text can be used with any of the informational text standards as a standalone text or through excerpts as an accompaniment to a related social studies unit.

Young, Black, and Determined: A Biography of Lorraine Hansberry
Patricia McKissack and Frederick McKissack
ISBN: 978-0823413003

The McKissacks have a long history of crafting biographies that celebrate African-American and minority figures. With a blend of colorful language and important facts, the text presents the seldom-told story of Hansberry's contribution to the American canon and her struggles in life. This text offers numerous opportunities for students to connect ideas, events, and individuals while considering author's viewpoint and word choices.

Digital/ Online Text

American Rhetoric Paired Speeches

http://www.americanrhetoric.com/top100speechesall.html

The top one hundred speeches of all time have been compiled based on a list created by Dr. Stephen Lucas and Dr. Martin Medhurst of the University of Wisconsin at Madison. The majority of the speeches are available for students to listen to (audio) and read as a .pdf file. This provides two different formats of the same text to analyze. I suggest pulling the links and text yourself. Recently the site has started to feature advertisements that can be distracting to students. My favorite speeches for analysis include:

- *Checkers*, **Richard M. Nixon**
- *Civil Rights Address*, **John F. Kennedy**
- *I Have a Dream*, **Martin Luther King, Jr.**
- *We Shall Overcome*, **Lyndon B. Johnson**
- *1981 Presidential Inaugural Address*, **Ronald Reagan**
- *Resignation Address to the Nation*, **Richard Nixon**

Bottled Water is Silly — But So is Banning It
Charles Fishman

http://newswatch.nationalgeographic.com/2012/02/13/bottled-water-is-silly-but-so-is-banning-it/

This *National Geographic* article discusses bottled water use. The author presents a nuanced argument and is a bit tongue-in-cheek. The author's tone and his word choices are worth discussing. Students get to see an example of an informational text that also has a clear voice.

New York Times Global Warming Archive

http://topics.nytimes.com/top/news/science/topics/globalwarming/index.html

This is the *New York Times* archive of global warming articles. This source provides a wealth of different articles on global warming. It lists them in reverse chronological order, providing easy access to the most recent. I find that these articles present a clear point of view and offer excellent examples of claims, evidence, and varying word choices.

Contemporary

Conversations with America
Julia Alvarez

http://weekendamerica.publicradio.org/display/web/2008/11/01/conversations_alvarez/

This is possibly the shortest text included on the suggested text list. This brief essay-style article features Alvarez explaining what the right to vote means to her. She uses her own experiences and quotes to voice her feelings about voting. This piece is an excellent companion for any social studies unit on voting rights or the electoral process.

Chew On This: Everything You Don't Want to Know About Fast Food
Charles Wilson and Eric Schlosser
ISBN: 978-0618593941
This book explores the dangers of fast food and obesity. Humorous, yet disturbing at the same time, the text offers a high level of engagement while focusing on a serious topic. An adaptation of Schlosser's *Fast Food Nation*, this informational text offers a strong tone and point of view about the fast food industry.

Geeks: How Two Lost Boys Rode the Internet out of Idaho
John Katz
ISBN: 978-0767906999
Katz, a journalist, details his correspondence with teen hackers, Jesse and Eric. As a self-proclaimed geek, Katz explores the complicated nature and evolution of geeks. Exploring issues of self-acceptance, transformation, and identity, this text offers connections for any middle school student. Creative word choices and accounts of painful and gratifying experiences help craft an understanding of geekhood and the eventual "Geek Ascension" of each character.

Knots in My Yo-Yo String
Jerry Spinelli
ISBN: 978-0679887911
Spinelli (*Crash, Loser,* and *Maniac Magee*) will be a familiar name to many middle school students. In this 160-page autobiography, he paints a picture of his life experiences with the same style he uses in his fiction books. Spinelli focuses on how he grew to become a writer. The conversational tone will hold the interest of most students and encourage your would-be future writers to hold tightly to their pens.

The Digital Divide
Mark Bauerlein
ISBN: 978-1585428861
This is an excellent source for any teacher focusing on the evaluation of argument. Bauerlein's text includes essays written by a wide variety of authors. Each essay focuses on the relationship that the younger generation has to technology and digital communication. Each essay is organized by subtopics. Many of the pieces have been published before and offer great opportunities for analysis of author viewpoint, wordplay, perspectives, and supporting reasons. This is a particularly good choice for examining the evidence that each author provides to support specific claims.

The Struggle to be an All-American Girl
Elizabeth Wong
Los Angeles Times, 1980 (Can be purchased from latimes.org online archive)
Full text is also easily found on the Internet.
This essay walks readers through the challenges that the author had growing up balancing the competing demands of being Chinese and her perceptions of being an American. Written from a teen perspective, the text offers a raw, honest perception of childhood desires and developing images of self. Students have several opportunities to draw inferences about the narrator and central ideas, as well as to make multiple extensions and connections.

124

Travels with Charley in Search of America
John Steinbeck
ISBN: 978-0140053203

This 300-page travel diary is written in narrative style. Steinbeck and his dog, Charley, travel across America to explore the country. Steinbeck explains his motive for wanting to embark on this journey and presents a clear tone and point of view as he explores multiple towns and cities. The book has a wide variety of emotional moments. One challenge is that this text may seem disjointed to middle school students because it can seem more like a collection of disparate experiences, rather than a more linear memoir.

Yell-Oh Girls! Emerging Voices Explore Culture, Identity, and Growing Up Asian-American
Vickie Nam
ISBN: 0060959444

This text explores issues of identity formation through the 80 essays written by mostly teen writers. Most selections are under three pages, and a few letters and poems are included as well. Most appropriate for older eighth graders and even high school students, this text offers powerful examples of point of view and author's perspective. These essays, on subjects such as language, feminism, stereotypes, and adoption, work well when paired with units that explore identity, the American Dream, or diversity. I do not suggest using this as a whole, but rather select the individual essays that are appropriate for your unit of study or class. There are some sensitive topics that you will need to preview carefully for age appropriateness.

125

Beyond Text

"There are two people in every photograph: the photographer and the viewer."

Ansel Adams, photographer

READING INFORMATIONAL TEXT STANDARD 7:
BEYOND TEXT

Sixth	Seventh	Eighth
Integrate information presented in different media or formats (e.g., visually, quantitatively) as well as in words to develop a coherent understanding of a topic or issue.	Compare and contrast a text to an audio, video, or multimedia version of the text, analyzing each medium's portrayal of the subject (e.g., how the delivery of a speech affects the impact of the words).	Evaluate the advantages and disadvantages of using different mediums (e.g., print or digital text, video, multimedia) to present a particular topic or idea.

GRADE LEVEL DIFFERENCES

While each of the standards relate to different types of multimodal text, each grade level has a different level of rigor. Sixth graders are tasked with looking at information presented in different formats to understand an issue or topic. Seventh graders will focus on contrasting multimodal text to determine how the formats impact the subject or message. Eighth graders will go a step further and make some judgment calls about the different formats. They will compare formats and think about the pros and cons of the different mediums.

6th grade: Use information from two different formats to understand one topic or issue.
7th grade: Compare and contrast how different types of media communicate about a subject.
8th grade: Evaluate the pros and cons of different mediums to present about a subject or idea.

Key Point

"Reading" text is no longer just about print. Students can "read" images, audio, and multimedia.

Beyond Text needs to be introduced after standards one through six. Why? This standard is about looking at what you have already read, then integrating and evaluating content from a different medium or source. The more adept students are at analyzing information, the easier this standard will be. Students should use what they have learned about the Central Ideas and the Word Play standards to evaluate meaning from different types of text. The focus here is on moving beyond print text and evaluating multimodal text.

The increased rigor from sixth to eighth grade can be understood as steps in a continuum. Each step is placed in one grade level and they build sequentially in terms of rigor.

► **The first step (6th grade) is to simply gather information from more than one source or medium.**

► **The second step (7th grade) is to look critically at the information presented through those sources to compare and contrast them.**

► **The final step (8th grade) is to make judgments about the mediums and their presentations.**

In order to effectively teach this standard, you need to have a keen awareness of what counts as moving beyond the text. This standard is about focusing on two different forms of text that can stand alone. Examining a chart, graph, or image within a text may be a useful practice, but it falls outside of the aims of this standard. For example, a student could compare the movie to the book. Each can stand alone and be considered a distinct piece of its own. A student could examine a stage play compared to the written drama. The transcript of a speech could be compared to watching the person actually deliver the speech. These are just a few examples to contextualize the concept of moving beyond the text.

The simplest point of entry for this standard is to look at the wording for the seventh-grade standard and work with a set of paired sources that present the exact same content. This way the focus can be on exactly how the formats or mediums influence the message. The suggested text list is organized in pairs for precisely this reason.

While this standard may appear to be an easier or lighter standard compared to others, it is one of the most relevant to the ways that students gather information today. This standard is one that traditionally has not been given a great deal of focus within traditional language and reading courses. With the constantly changing modes of communication and the abundance of audio, visual, and multimedia information available for consumption, this standard grows increasingly more relevant.

1 Lead a discussion with your students about how they find out new information. Encourage them to think about how they gather information for things that are important to them. *"How do you find out information when you want to figure something out or learn something new?"*

2 Record their ideas on the board. When you have a variety of mediums included, stop and review the list. Label which ones use audio, multimedia, or visual elements.

3 Introduce the lesson objectives. *"Today we will talk about how to compare and contrast information that you find from different types of sources and use it to learn about topics just like you do in your real lives every day."*

4 Explain the task for this standard. *"We are going to move beyond just reading books and take a look at information that you can see, hear, or interact with."*

5 Share the standard with students and introduce key vocabulary that they will encounter. There is no magic formula for introducing the vocabulary. Use what works in your class normally. The important part is that students understand the literal definition of each word.

Common Core Buzzword

Use the language of the standards when discussing vocabulary:

Audio

Visual

Multimedia

Media

Source

Medium

Format

129

INSTRUCTIONAL VARIATIONS:

▸ **Vocabulary can be introduced in advance. This allows you to move directly to practice or to model additional examples.**

▸ **Vocabulary can be done at the beginning of the lesson as the opener.**

▸ **A Frayer Model or word sort can be used to simply explore the different vocabulary words of the standard.**

1 **Before beginning this model lesson, select a topic that you can share text, images, charts, or videos about.** You want to choose a topic that has at least three of the components. I really like to use the *History Channel* website (see suggested text list) for this activity.

2 **Explain that you decided to do research on a specific topic.** *"I decided to do a little research on (your topic of choice). I want to show you how I compared information from different mediums."*

3 **Pull up the website and share the text, images, video (always a fun choice), or graphics associated with your topic.** You want to simply look at each piece, review the content, and discuss what you note about each.

4 **Lead a discussion about how these sources are different.** The goal is to get students to find value in each format. For example, a video clip may provide a certain perspective, but the text may offer specific facts and details that other mediums miss.

5 **Collaboratively discuss your sources, noting characteristics of each.** Work together to create a three-column T-chart to compare each source like the anchor chart pictured below. Ask students to consider this same process when they compare mediums and information. Post the chart in an accessible location.

130

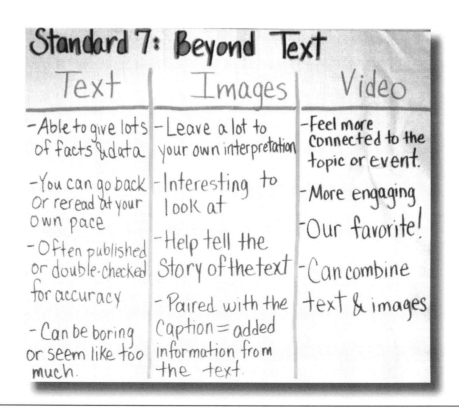

THE ORGANIZERS

Once you have explicitly introduced and modeled how to apply the strategies of the standard, now is the time to shift gears and provide students with multiple opportunities to practice the skill with their own reading in pairs, groups, and independently.

The Beyond Text standard requires text from multiple mediums on the same topic. You will notice that the suggested text list for this chapter is organized by topic. For these organizers we used a video interview (*Tap Water Versus Bottled Water?*), a news article (*Five Reasons Not to Drink Bottled Water*), and a consumer fact sheet (*Tap Water, Bottled Water, Filtered Water: Which to Choose?*). You can select any combination of texts to model this for students as long as they include different mediums.

1 Read or view each of the selections with students. If you don't have a copy for each student, project the text so that all students can read it. Model how to complete the organizer using the samples that I have modeled next to each organizer or complete your own sample from the blank copy found in each section.

2 Once you model by explicitly completing the organizer yourself, your students will see the connection between the informational text and the organizer. You can provide blank copies of the organizer and allow students to select their own informational text, assign one from your class anthology, or select a title from the suggested book list within this chapter.

3 Students can complete the organizer with any combination of multimodal informational text. This can be done as an assignment and can be repeated as many times as you want with different sets of informational text. The sky is the limit! This allows for multiple opportunities to tailor the text to the student and maintain fidelity to the standard.

4 Once students have demonstrated mastery of the skill, don't stop using it. You want them to keep practicing. In the introduction of the book, I discussed the pitfalls of being a Checklist Teacher. Students need to keep perfecting their skill sets.

5 Reuse the same organizer, make it into an anchor chart, or post exemplars for students to reference later. You can reuse the organizers for multiple practice opportunities and formative assessments. The goal is for students to be able to use the organizers to think about text independently.

131

COLOR CODING

Assign each one a different color. I like to use corresponding highlighter colors: pink, yellow, green, etc.

Model this organizer using familiar text that students have already reviewed and understand.

Color Coding

Topic: Bottled Water Industry

Source #1	Source #2	Source #3
MSNBC Interview	5 Reasons not to drink Bottled Water	Tap Water, Bottled Water, Filtered Water?
Format	**Format**	**Format**
Interview	News Article	Fact Sheet
☐ Color	☐ Color	☐ Color
What I Learned	**What I Learned**	**What I Learned**
Consumers have no choice over tap providers, but they choose BW providers. CHOICE	Bottle water is really about $$ and marketing.	There are easy & low cost ways to improve tap water

Summary (Color Code Sources) Bottled water is a huge industry that makes many companies profitable. Despite this, there are cheap & easy ways to get the same water. In the end, however, it is the consumer who makes the choice!!

After the summary, ask students to highlight or underline in the corresponding color which source informed their summaries.

The Common Core Guidebook, 6-8: Informational Text Lessons

Color Coding

©2013 The Common Core Guidebook. Intended for classroom use only. May not be reproduced or distributed without permission.

Topic:

Source #1

Format

☐ Color

What I Learned

Source #2

Format

☐ Color

What I Learned

Source #3

Format

☐ Color

What I Learned

Summary (Color Code Sources)

COMPARING SOURCES

Venn diagrams can easily
be adapted to include more
than two topics or sources.

I used the MSNBC
YouTube interview here.

I used the Five Reasons
Not to Drink Bottled
Water article here.

Comparing Sources

Interview
Source #1

Article
Source #2

Seeing the people
made it more
emotional & it
seemed like a
'bigger deal'

Regulation
is different
for both types of
water.

Evidence &
data in print
seemed to
have a bigger
impact.
(1.5 million tons)

People make a
choice to drink
BW. They should
investigate &
call the
companies.

Bottled water is
not looked at
in the same
way so
TW.

Tap water is
regulated &
fine to drink.

What I Learned:

The are different levels of regulation between TW
and BW. BW is considered a food product and the
consumers are charged with choosing or not choosing.

After you model the Venn diagram,
ask students to use the organizer
to complete the "What I Learned"
section. Discuss and compare.

Many students will start to
get confused with the differences
& similarities. They may just
start listing facts. Consider
using different colors for the
similarities & differences.

©2013 The Common Core Guidebook. Intended for classroom use only. May not be reproduced or distributed without permission.

Comparing Sources

Source #1

Source #2

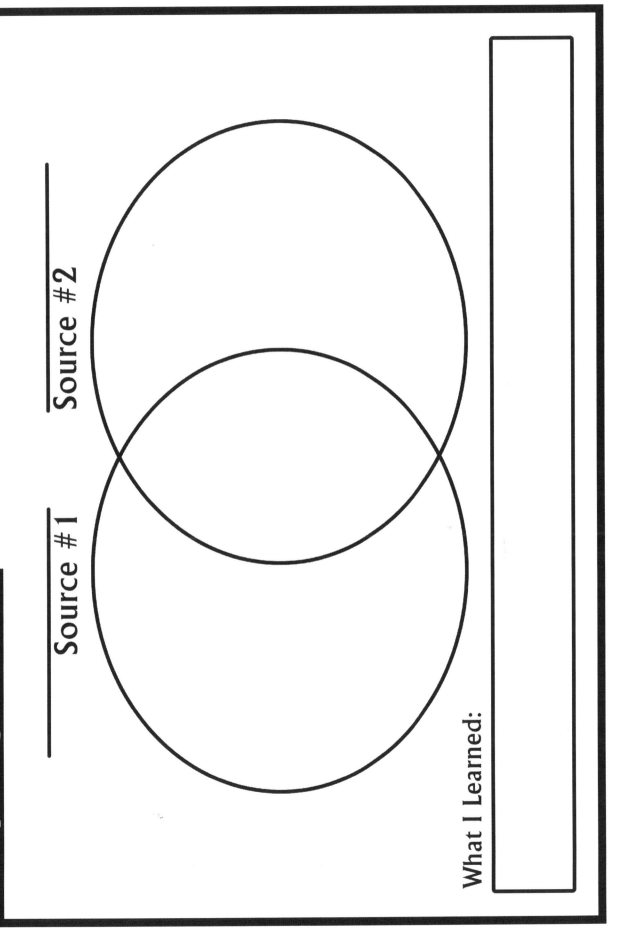

What I Learned:

WHICH MEDIUM?

Use this as a general anchor chart about the different mediums or just how they are used with specific topics.

Encourage students to talk back to the text through questions.

Which Medium?

	Audio	Video	Multimedia	Text
Pros	A good reader can use lots of intonation to encourage attentiveness	The emotion and facial expressions are evident.	Can use multiple devices: – video – hyperlinks – images – text	Can refer back and review the sections as you choose. Take notes!
Cons	Without a transcript in front of you, can be easy to get off track.	Often cannot read the facts. The pro can be a con too.	Can be confusing or too busy. Information overload?	Have to pay attention to subtle word choice differences for POV.
Examples	Speeches Podcasts	MSNBC Interviews People on 20/20 & news	Interactive Websites history.com	News articles Biographies Op-eds Nonfiction

Extend the Thinking

I like to do 'mini debates' where students take on the persona of one medium & present their case for why they are the most effective & informative.

136

©2013 The Common Core Guidebook. Intended for classroom use only. May not be reproduced or distributed without permission.

Which Medium?

	Audio	Video	Multimedia	Text
Pros				
Cons				
Examples				

To effectively work on this standard, teachers need multiple formats of text on the same topic. Select a topic first and match two different text, audio, visual, or multimedia formats for analysis. To meet this standard, the suggested text list for this section is organized in sets. Each topic includes at least two different formats of text on the topic identified.

AUDIO AND WRITTEN SPEECHES

American Rhetoric Paired Speeches

http://www.americanrhetoric.com/top100speechesall.html

The top one hundred speeches of all time have been compiled based on a list created by Dr. Stephen Lucas and Dr. Martin Medhurst of the University of Wisconsin at Madison. The majority of the speeches are available for students to listen to (audio) and read as a .pdf file. This provides two different formats of the same text to analyze. I suggest pulling the links and text yourself. Recently the site has started to feature advertisements that can be distracting to students. My favorite speeches for analysis include:

- ► *Checkers,* **Richard M. Nixon**
- ► *Civil Rights Address,* **John F. Kennedy**
- ► *I Have a Dream,* **Martin Luther King, Jr.**
- ► *We Shall Overcome,* **Lyndon B. Johnson**
- ► *1981 Presidential Inaugural Address,* **Ronald Reagan**
- ► *Resignation Address to the Nation,* **Richard Nixon**

BOTTLED WATER CONSUMPTION

Five Reasons Not to Drink Bottled Water

Chris Baskind

http://www.mnn.com/food/healthy-eating/stories/5-reasons-not-to-drink-bottled-water

The article makes the argument that bottled water is no better than tap water. The author presents five key reasons why consumers should opt for water from the tap over bottled choices. Exploring the role that marketing has on consumer decisions to purchase bottled water, the text is an excellent example of crafting an argument and supporting it with details.

Flow: For the Love of Water
Oscilloscope Pictures: 2006

This documentary paints a stark picture about the future of water availability. Focusing on the commercialization of water, the film traces how big business interests impact who owns and controls water sources.

News Interview: MSNBC: Tap Water versus Bottled Water?
http://www.youtube.com/watch?v=kZ74e_NitXU

This is an interview from 2009 where representatives from the tap water industry and the bottled water industry are interviewed. They discuss the differences between the two regulatory systems. The three-minute interview puts a voice and a face on the topic.

Tap Water, Bottled Water, Filtered Water: Which to Choose?
http://www.foodsafety.wisc.edu/consumer/fact_sheets/waterbottles.pdf

This article uses bullets, labeled images, and hyperlinks to present the pros and cons of each type of water. Presented in a simple, three-page format, this article is a straightforward example of an argument with support. The article explains factors that may influence the safety of tap water, along with the procedure for processing bottled water. This short article is a great piece to read with students and discuss the central ideas of the text and supporting evidence.

CAFFEINE CONSUMPTION

Caffeine: How Much is Too Much?
Mayo Clinic Staff
http://www.mayoclinic.com/health/caffeine/NU00600

This web article offers a wide variety of facts and warnings about caffeine. The article provides data organized in multiple ways; bulleted lists and cause/effect structures are used most frequently.

Ted Ed
Caffeine!! - Bite Sci-zed
Alex Dainis
http://ed.ted.com/on/gTGfE82A

This fast paced 5-minute video shows how caffeine works as an addictive stimulant. The speaker consumes two large coffee drinks during the broadcast to demonstrate the impact of the drug. Combined with images and data, the author provides an overload of information on the dangers of caffeine.

CLIMATE CHANGE

An Inconvenient Truth
Al Gore
Paramount: 2006
This now-famous documentary chronicles the consequences of global warming. Footage and interviews are used to make the case for increased awareness and action to help halt global warming. This documentary offers readers an excellent opportunity to examine word choice and evaluate evidence. I suggest using segments or clips with students.

Global Warming with Tom Brokaw
http://www.youtube.com/watch?v=xcVwLrAavyA
This is an hour-long television special on global warming. The broadcast features a wealth of facts, rhetoric, and interviews with climate scientists that students can use to evaluate as "text." What arguments are being made? What evidence is presented? How valid are these details? You can probably find this same video or clips of this video from numerous online sources.

Let's Prepare for Our New Climate
Vicki Arroyo
http://www.ted.com/talks/vicki_arroyo_let_s_prepare_for_our_new_climate.html
In this 15-minute talk Arroyo shares the impact of climate change on her family, including images of how she was personally impacted, larger-scale consequences, and the international impact of global warming. She provides multiple ways to prepare for life in a world with a shifting climate by offering a suggested list of actions in a problem/solution format.

New York Times Global Warming Archive
http://topics.nytimes.com/top/news/science/topics/globalwarming/index.html
This is the *New York Times* archive of global warming articles. This source offers a wealth of different articles on global warming. It lists them in reverse chronological order, providing easy access to the most recent. I find that these articles present a clear point of view and offer excellent examples of claims, evidence, and varying word choices.

The Sky's Not Falling! Why It's OK to Chill About Global Warming
Holly Fretwell
ISBN: 978-0976726944
Fretwell's controversial text is a counterargument to the claim that global warming is a critical problem. The author presents an argument that global warming is really not a concern and positions herself as the logical, balanced alternative to educational informational that just frightens people about global warming. Encouraging readers to "just chill," Fretwell insists that the media is simply indoctrinating teens with a false sense of urgency and fear.

Multiple Historical Topics

History Channel: Topics Feature
http://www.history.com/topics

This source could really stand alone for the Beyond Text standard. The website is organized to include videos, articles, images, and interactive media features related to over one hundred topics. Students can easily compare videos, images, articles, and interactive media from one location on a wide variety of topics. Some topics that seem interesting and well-rounded include:

- ▶ **Alexander Graham Bell**
- ▶ **American Revolution**
- ▶ **American Women in World War II**
- ▶ **Ancient Greece**
- ▶ **Boston Massacre**
- ▶ **Dred Scott Case**
- ▶ **Henry Ford**
- ▶ **Invention of the PC**
- ▶ **J. P. Morgan**
- ▶ **Julius Caesar**
- ▶ **Marie-Antoinette**
- ▶ **Mohandas Gandhi**
- ▶ **The Industrial Revolution**
- ▶ **The U. S. Constitution**
- ▶ **Titanic**

School Desegregation

Independent Lens: Daisy Bates: First Lady of Little Rock
2011 PBS Documentary
Available as a digital streaming video and PC download on Amazon Prime.

This 55-minute movie explores the life of Daisy Bates, a journalist and one of the original students to integrate Little Rock High School in 1964. Produced by PBS, the film handles sensitive issues with a delicate hand while still being true to the realities of this era.

Remember: The Journey to School Integration
Toni Morrison
ISBN: 978-0618397402

In this award-winning book, Morrison uses archival photographs to chronicle the school desegregation process. This visual collection provides a rich source of data and imagery, painting a vivid image of the struggles and challenges of this era.

Through My Eyes
Ruby Bridges and Margo Lundell
ISBN: 978-0590189231

This text follows Ruby Bridges as she becomes the first African-American student to integrate the New Orleans, Louisiana schools. Escorted by federal marshals, she experienced hatred and racism during a racially-charged movement. The book weaves a lucid image of racism and bigotry from a child's point of view and experiences. Note: This book uses the word *nigger*.

Warriors Don't Cry: A Searing Memoir of the Battle to Integrate Little Rock's Central High
Melba Pattillo Beals
ISBN: 978-1416948827

This is the abridged version of a text commonly read by high school and even college students. 100 pages shorter, this text is manageable for your older middle school students. The text is well-organized and provides a great deal of background information on the desegregation of Little Rock High School. Up close and personal experiences with being kicked, hit, and spit-upon are chronicled to paint a vivid picture of the injustices of this era. This text can be used with any of the informational text standards as a standalone text or through excerpts as an accompaniment to a related social studies unit.

STATES

10 Things You May Not Know About the US States
http://www.history.com/shows/how-the-states-got-their-shapes/articles/10-things-you-may-not-know-about-the-us-states

This article is really more of an extended bulleted list of fun facts about different states. Focusing on the shapes of states, this list is a fun, easy companion to a larger piece on state shapes (see Stein's book as an example).

How the States Got Their Shapes
http://www.history.com/shows/how-the-states-got-their-shapes/videos/playlists/full-episodes#how-the-states-got-their-shapes-the-great-plains-trains--automobiles

This website has a series of videos from the television show of the same name. Featuring videos that range from a half-hour to just over an hour, each video details how different shapes came to be. I suggest selecting a video about a particular region or state and pairing it with the same chapter in Stein's text. There are links to photo galleries of each state and additional clips from each show.

How the States Got Their Shapes
Mark Stein
ISBN: 978-0061431395

Stein's 350-page book, divided by state, presents facts and images to explain why states are shaped the way that they are. Some parts are written in narrative style, while others rely more on archival evidence to explain the rationale behind the various shapes. The text is easy to read and can be approached by state. Students can easily compare and contrast the shape origins between different states, or use the state chapters to supplement more targeted units of study across the curriculum.

Sugar & Artificial Sweeteners

Added Sugar: Don't Get Sabotaged by Sweeteners
Mayo Clinic Staff
http://www.mayoclinic.com/health/added-sugar/MY00845
Relying on headings, lists, definitions, and bold words, this two-page article is representative of the type of informational text students will readily encounter online. The article relies on a great deal of statistics to demonstrate the adverse effects of sugar.

Artificial Sweeteners: Sugar-free, but at What Cost?
Holly Strawbridge
http://www.health.harvard.edu/blog/artificial-sweeteners-sugar-free-but-at-what-cost-201207165030
This informational text article examines the effects of a sugar-free diet supplemented with artificial sweeteners. Relying on data from the American Heart Association and the American Diabetes Association, this article is rich with quotes and hyperlinks to additional data.

Dr. Keri Peterson on Dr. Oz "Artificial Sweeteners"
YouTube
https://www.youtube.com/watch?v=A-hUyw2lcio
This YouTube video discusses the impact of sugar substitutes. Presenting myth and fact, the six-minute segment provides a quick and easy to understand set of facts about aspartame, saccharin, and sucralose. Dr. Oz presents a series of questions and concerns about sugar alternatives to Dr. Keri Peterson. She argues that artificial sweeteners are safe. Be careful to review the associated videos or ads that may be included on the sidebars. There may be inappropriate links to videos or advertisements.

Titanic

Shadow of the Titanic: The Extraordinary Stories of Those Who Survived
Andrew Wilson
ISBN: 978-1451671568
This text is based on the diaries, memories, letters, and interviews of the surviving members of the Titanic. Students can read specific chapters that follow individual survivors. The chapters chronicle how they remember that fateful day and how they coped after the event. Filled with colorful language, this text can be used in multiple ways to model the informational text standards.

Titanic in Photographs (Titanic Collection)
Daniel Klistorner, Steve Hall, Bruce Beveridge, Art Braunschweiger, Scott Andrews, and Ken Marschall
ISBN: 978-0752458960
This 168-page book features images of the Titanic, many never published before. Organized to tell the story of the Titanic visually, this book offers students the visual aspect that the Beyond Text standard calls for in the sixth and eighth grade. This book can be paired with an informational text that recounts the Titanic or a website that does the same.

Evaluating Evidence

"To argue with a person who has renounced the use of reason is like administering medicine to the dead."
Thomas Paine, *The Crisis*

Reading Informational Text Standard 8: EVALUATING EVIDENCE

Sixth	Seventh	Eighth
Trace and evaluate the argument and specific claims in a text, distinguishing claims that are supported by reasons and evidence from claims that are not.	Trace and evaluate the argument and specific claims in a text, assessing whether the reasoning is sound and the evidence is relevant and sufficient to support the claims.	Delineate and evaluate the argument and specific claims in a text, assessing whether the reasoning is sound and the evidence is relevant and sufficient; recognize when irrelevant evidence is introduced.

GRADE LEVEL DIFFERENCES

Each grade level has the same core focus: evaluating arguments and supporting evidence. In sixth grade, students need to be able to look for claims and classify them as being supported by evidence or not. The primary focus is making sure that students can recognize the argument and determine if support is there. In seventh grade, students will continue to do this, but now they are tasked with determining if the evidence is sufficient enough to support the claims. In the eighth grade they perform the same task, but determine if any irrelevant evidence has been added.

Evaluating Evidence is one of the more multifaceted standards that students will encounter. This standard requires that students can find an argument, determine if and how that argument is supported, and make evaluative claims about the strength of the evidence.

This standard also directly ties in with argument writing. The same skill set required to evaluate evidence is the same skill set required when teaching students to write an argument piece. When students craft an argument piece, they need to make claims and support them with valid reasons and evidence. For this informational text standard, Evaluating Evidence, students are asked to look at another piece of writing and assess what the author did.

While this is an informational text standard, teachers need to consider the structure and information needed for writing. The same introduction and modeling used here can also be used to introduce argument writing. In fact, the very same informational texts that students read can become mentor texts to consider for their own writing organization.

It is important to notice that this standard, while an informational text standard, is about looking specifically at informational text that makes a claim,

asks the reader to take action, or is persuasive in nature. While I believe that everything is an argument, narrative nonfiction is probably not the best choice for the introduction of this standard. When you plan for explicit instruction, you want to select pieces that give the most clearly articulated examples of what you want to model. News articles, magazines, and commentary pieces are well-suited to offer students multiple ways to interrogate text and look for evidence. The suggested text list includes options that meet these criteria.

It is also very useful to draw connections to Textual Evidence (standard one) here. Students have already been looking for evidence to support their own inferences and claims about text. For the Evaluating Evidence standard, students are taking a different role. Instead of looking for textual evidence, in general, to support their own inferences, they are evaluating if the author has supplied enough evidence and reasons within the text to support his or her own claims.

Writing Connection

The more that students can see the evidence in other writing, the more effective they will be when they are tasked with writing their own informational text, supported by evidence.

Key Point

Evaluation and synthesis are higher-level critical thinking skills that students can and should apply across the curriculum. Draw from rich science and social studies sources. The Evaluating Evidence standard moves far beyond just a 'reading' skill. This is a thinking skill.

146

1 **Lead a discussion by asking students to name a few dramas, detective, or law shows.** Possible responses: *CSI, Scandal, Damages, Law & Order,* etc. "*Has anyone ever seen one of those lawyer or police dramas on television?*"

2 "*One of my favorite parts of any show like that is when they try to prove if someone is innocent or guilty. How do they usually decide if someone is guilty? What makes the difference?*" Solicit responses. Possible responses: testimony, witnesses, evidence, video, etc.

3 **Focus on the fact that they need to have evidence to prove their points on these shows.** Evidence supports their judgments.

4 "*What about when they have evidence, but the criminal gets away? Have you seen that happen when the person is guilty, they had evidence, but the jury or judge didn't believe the evidence?*" Lead students to the conclusion that not all evidence is equal. Sometimes evidence is there, but it is not strong enough, doesn't seem as convincing, or just doesn't really relate to the case.

5 "*I like to hold writers to the same standards that they use on those shows. I want to see the evidence.*" Discuss how newspapers and magazines feature text where people state a wide variety of things, but a good reader should look at the evidence and decide if the argument the writer is making has sufficient support.

6 "*We will spend some time looking critically at what authors say. You and I will be the judge and jury. We will decide if there is enough evidence to support what these authors are saying.*"

7 **Introduce vocabulary words to students and explain that everyone will use these words when they discuss evidence in informational text.**

Key Vocabulary:

Argument – what are you saying?

Claim – what are you saying?

Evidence – what proof do you have?

Reasons – why should I believe your claim?

Support – what evidence & reasons prove your argument?

Sufficient – did you provide enough support or reasons for your claim to make sense?

147

1 **Make photocopies of a story from a tabloid magazine.** Make sure that the article you select is outlandish, appropriate to show middle school students, and has some type of evidence. Typical tabloid evidence includes anonymous sources or questionable photos.

2 **Make a connection to how students already use evidence to prove what they think or understand about a text.** *"Authors should do the same thing when they make an argument or claim."*

3 **Explain to students that they will focus on examining argument writing.** *"We will spend some time looking at argument writing. These pieces will all feature authors who are attempting to prove their point about a topic. Our jobs will be to look at the evidence they give us and determine if it is sufficient enough to support their claims."*

4 **Distribute the copy of the tabloid article.** These can be copies or an interactive whiteboard projection.

5 **Ask students to think about what argument or claim the author is making.** They should try to think like a lawyer and analyze what kinds of evidence the authors have presented to support their claims.

6 **Read the text aloud together.** Stop frequently to make comments and think out loud to show your thinking about the article.

7 **After you have read the article, discuss the value of the evidence and whether or not the students think that it provided sufficient support for the argument.**

8 **Distribute a second text (from the suggested list or from your own collection) to your students and repeat the same procedure.** News articles with lots of statistics are excellent for this purpose.

9 **Compare how the second piece had a lot more evidence and reasons to support the author's claims.** *"How can we compare the evidence used in these two articles? How are they different?"*

THE ORGANIZERS

Once you have explicitly introduced and modeled how to apply the strategies of the standard, now is the time to shift gears and provide students with multiple opportunities to practice the skill with their own reading in pairs, groups, and independently.

Students always need models, so each organizer has been completed based on *Five Reasons Not to Drink Bottled Water* by Chris Baskind. This particular text is used for each example under the Evaluating Evidence standard for consistency and to offer the same text as a point of comparison for teachers.

1 Read (or reread) the article with students. Model how to complete the organizer using the samples that I have modeled next to each organizer or complete your own sample from the blank copy found in each section.

2 Once you model by explicitly completing the organizer yourself, your students will see the connection between the informational text and the organizer. You can provide blank copies of the organizer and allow students to select their own informational text, assign one from your class anthology, or select a title from the suggested book list within this chapter.

3 Students can complete the organizer when they read any informational text. This can be done as an assignment and can be repeated as many times as you want with any informational text that you choose. The sky is the limit! This allows for multiple opportunities to tailor the text to the student and maintain fidelity to the standard.

4 Once students have demonstrated mastery of the skill, don't stop using it. You want them to keep practicing. In the introduction of the book, I discussed the pitfalls of being a Checklist Teacher. Students need to keep perfecting their skill sets.

5 Reuse the same organizer, make it into an anchor chart, or post exemplars for students to reuse the organizers for multiple practice opportunities and formative assessments. The goal is for students to be able to use the organizers to think about text independently.

149

CLAIMS & EVIDENCE

create an anchor chart
modeled after this
organizer for students
to refer to with all
informational text.

💡 Extend the
Thinking

Scaffold this for struggling readers by
cutting the organizer into thirds & having
students look for one claim at a time.

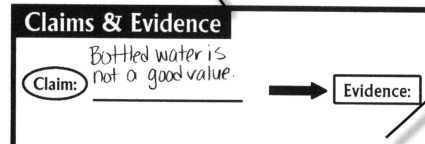

Claims & Evidence

Claim: Bottled water is
not a good value.
_____

→ **Evidence:** BW: 5¢ an ounce
Tw: 1¢ a gallon

Claim: Bottled water is
≠ healthier
_____

→ **Evidence:** Less health
regulations on BW

Claim: Bottled water =
lots of waste
_____

→ **Evidence:** 1.5 million tons
of plastic annually.

This organizer works
well with **science** and
social studies content.

Point out the connection to
Standard 1: Textual Evidence.
This is really simply an
extension.

150

Claims & Evidence

©2013 The Common Core Guidebook. Intended for classroom use only. May not be reproduced or distributed without permission.

Claim: _____ → **Evidence:** _____

Claim: _____ → **Evidence:** _____

Claim: _____ → **Evidence:** _____

CLAIM CYCLE

Writing Connection

Student can use this organizer as a brainstorming tool for a written analysis paper or article response.

Claim Cycle

Claim

Water is becoming a commercial entity. It is being taken over by business.

Reason or Evidence

Multinational companies are buying most groundwater & distribution rights.

How Sound/Strong is the Evidence?

- No #s to show how many
- No hyperlinks to verify source

My Decision on This Claim

Unsure if it is valid. Need to check other sources for validity of claim.

Common Core Buzzword

Introduce generalizable language related to arguments: validity, claim, sound, & verify.

Students have to rely on critical thinking to evaluate the strength of the evidence.

©2013 The Common Core Guidebook. Intended for classroom use only. May not be reproduced or distributed without permission.

Claim Cycle

Reason or Evidence

Claim

How Sound/Strong is the Evidence?

My Decision on This Claim

ARGUMENT PYRAMID

Writing
Connection

Excellent brainstorming organizer for developing student argument papers as well.

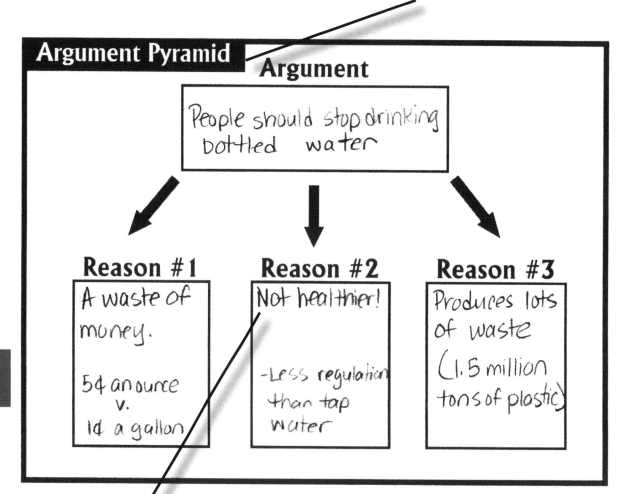

Argument Pyramid

Argument

People should stop drinking bottled water

Reason #1

A waste of money.

5¢ an ounce
v.
1¢ a gallon

Reason #2

Not healthier!

-Less regulation than tap water

Reason #3

Produces lots of waste (1.5 million tons of plastic)

Highlighting evidence (reasons) in the text together before you model the actual completion of the organizer is a great way to show the mental steps that you take when thinking about evidence.

Argument Pyramid

©2013 The Common Core Guidebook. Intended for classroom use only. May not be reproduced or distributed without permission.

Argument

Reason #1

Reason #2

Reason #3

SOUND OR NOT?

One of my favorite choices for argument analysis! Students have lots of space to explain & defend their choices.

Sound or Not?	5 Reasons Not to Drink Bottled Water	
Argument	**Evidence**	**Sound or Not?**
Commodizing of water	Corporations are buying groundwater	No data #s, No links or source info. included = NOT
BW is not healthier	Cites FDA regulation rules.	Can look up. FDA is only federal- what about state BW=SOUND
Waste is much higher w/ BW	1.5 million tons of plastic 47 million gallons of oil used	Sources & Links w/ data SOUND

Abbreviations & symbols are okay! You are teaching & focusing on content, not artificial length or measures of work.

When you model this, consider selecting evidence that does not support the argument. Talk with students about how you reconcile or adjust your choices.

Sound or Not?

©2013 The Common Core Guidebook. Intended for classroom use only. May not be reproduced or distributed without permission.

Argument	Evidence	Sound or Not?

ANTHOLOGIES/BOOKS WITH MULTIPLE STORIES

Gutsy Girls
Tina Schwager and Michele Schuerger
ISBN: 978-1575420592

This is one of my favorite anthologies to use with young adults. The text is a compilation of 25 stories about women, mostly unknown, who have done something bold and exciting. Featuring college football players, rock climbers, marathon swimmers, and a host of athletes, this text will appeal to your sports fanatics, both male and female. The book does a good job of celebrating Girl Power while showing some nontraditional roles for women. Students can practice any of the standards with this text.

Teens Write Through It: Essays from Teens Who've Triumphed over Trouble
Fairview Press
ISBN: 978-1577490838

This collection of essays offers a powerful example of published teen writing. Each essay is crafted to share the experiences and lesson or central ideas taken away from the experiences. The authentic voices and easily relatable topics are effective at engaging preteen and teen readers.

Under Our Skin: Kids Talk about Race
Debbie Birdseye and Tom Birdseye
ISBN: 978-0823413256

Students share their perceptions of race in America. Told from the perspective of 12- and 13-year-olds, the text offers a candid peek into the multiplicity of experiences in America. Students have an opportunity to hear the voices of students their own age as they consider an issue often reserved for adults only.

FULL-LENGTH BOOKS

Chew On This: Everything You Don't Want to Know About Fast Food
Charles Wilson and Eric Schlosser
ISBN: 978-0618593941

This book explores the dangers of fast food and obesity. Humorous, yet disturbing at the same time, the text offers a high level of engagement while focusing on a serious topic. An adaptation of Schlosser's *Fast Food Nation*, this informational text offers a strong tone and point of view about the fast food industry.

The Digital Divide
Mark Bauerlein
ISBN: 978-1585428861

This is an excellent source for any teacher focusing on the evaluation of argument. Bauerlein's text includes essays written by a wide variety of authors. Each essay focuses on the relationship that the younger generation has to technology and digital communication. Each essay is organized by subtopics. Many of the pieces have been published before and offer great opportunities for analysis of author viewpoint, wordplay, perspectives, and supporting reasons. This is a particularly good choice for examining the evidence that each author provides to support specific claims.

The Ultimate Storm Survival Handbook
Warren Faidley
ISBN: 9781401602857

This handbook provides a wealth of facts about storms themselves, the damage they cause, and how to prepare in case of one. The text presents numerous claims with varying degrees of evidence to support the statements. Students are often engaged with the topic and eager to consider the suggestions and arguments put forth by Faidley.

ONLINE TEXT

Five Reasons Not to Drink Bottled Water
Chris Baskind
http://www.mnn.com/food/healthy-eating/stories/5-reasons-not-to-drink-bottled-water

The article makes the argument that bottled water is no better than tap water. The author presents five key reasons why consumers should opt for water from the tap over bottled choices. Exploring the role that marketing has on consumer decisions to purchase bottled water, the text is an excellent example of crafting an argument and supporting it with details.

35 Ancient Pyramids Discovered in Sudan Necropolis
Owen Jarvis
http://www.livescience.com/26903-35-ancient-pyramids-sudan.html

This article is a quick and simple text to read. Despite this, there are numerous opportunities to close read and consider the evidence, claims, and arguments that the author is making. Students have a wealth of informational text features such as photographs, related hyperlinks, and images to navigate as they read.

Picasso's Genius Revealed: He Used Common House Paint
Clara Moskowitz
http://www.livescience.com/26963-picasso-house-paint-x-rays.html

This news article makes the argument that Picasso did not use traditional artists' paint for his masterpieces. The text makes a claim and provides a wide variety of evidence to support the claim. This is a clear-cut and direct text that students can experiment with to analyze evidence.

159

Study: Facebook Teaches Kids Freedom of Speech
Ruth Manuel-Logan
http://allfacebook.com/study-facebook-teaches-kids-freedom-of-speech_b58683
This article is a brief news piece that supports the use of Facebook for students. The article presents a wide range of evidence that Facebook provides an appreciation of free speech in a way that school does not.

The Great Homework Debate: Is Homework Helpful or Harmful to Students?
Cory Ames
http://www.scilearn.com/blog/homework-debate-is-homework-helpful-or-harmful.php
This article looks at homework from a neutral position. The author evaluates the purpose and structure of homework assignments in school. Hyperlinks and references to sources are included, making this is an excellent informational text to examine for evidence.

Different Viewpoints

"There are no facts, only interpretations."
Friedrich Nietzsche, philosopher

Reading Informational Text Standard 9:
DIFFERENT VIEWPOINTS

Sixth	Seventh	Eighth
Compare and contrast one author's presentation of events with that of another (e.g., a memoir written by and a biography on the same person).	Analyze how two or more authors writing about the same topic shape their presentations of key information by emphasizing the different evidence or advancing different interpretations of facts.	Analyze a case in which two or more texts provide conflicting information on the same topic and identify where the texts disagree on matters of fact or interpretation.

GRADE LEVEL DIFFERENCES

A common misconception with this standard is that students only need to identify the author's purpose or the type of narration used (first person, third person). This is an unfortunate misread. In sixth grade, students are expected to determine the author's purpose or viewpoint and show specifically how the text is developed to communicate this. In seventh and eighth grade, students are expected to move beyond the simple identification of point of view and its development. The standard demands that students evaluate how the author addresses counterclaims and opposing viewpoints.

The skill set required for the Different Viewpoints standard is directly tied to the objectives of Evaluating Evidence (standard eight). If your students have not been introduced to the Evaluating Evidence standard, you may want to consider introducing it just before this unit.

The Evaluating Evidence standard focuses on helping students find an argument, determine if and how that argument is supported, and make evaluative claims about the strength of the evidence. Students will need that skill set to understand the Different Viewpoints standard. Now that they can evaluate evidence, they are tasked with effectively evaluating a second informational text selection (on the same topic or concept). After students analyze the arguments, they are expected to compare the arguments and evidence to those found in a second piece of text.

Whew! That is a mouthful and a handful for any student. To find success here, students need to have explicit practice comparing ideas, events, and people, as they are presented by each author.

To teach this standard you need a set of paired readings that explore the same topic or at least similar subject matter. The Different Viewpoints standard focuses on students being able to look at two or more texts and identify similarities and differences in how the information is presented. This standard is probably the most reliant on critical thinking and analysis.

Sixth graders focus on simple compare and contrast skills about a person or a specific topic. In the seventh grade, students expand their focus to more than two texts. This grade level is also tasked with considering how different authors focus on varying types of evidence that shape the presentation of their content. Eighth graders will continue this evaluation, but their examination is deliberately on paired texts with conflicting or opposing information.

As you prepare to teach this standard, you have three basic goals for your students. All of your lessons and practice opportunities should focus on:

► **Understanding the difference between compare and contrast**

► **Identifying evidence in text**

► **Understanding what interpretation means**

To examine how texts vary in their presentation of information, students can use Venn diagrams to look for similarities and differences. This is an organizer than many teachers have used with success. The challenge is to get students to read closely. Close rereading and analysis is quite useful and effective for this standard. Asking students to make annotations in the margins or use sticky notes is an effective strategy to get them to document their thinking.

Key Point

You don't teach students *what* to think or which viewpoint to endorse. You do teach them to evaluate and look for these differences on their own. The value is in students recognizing that there are different ways that authors position themselves and craft their own perspectives.

162

INTRODUCE *Different Viewpoints*

I begin this type of lesson with a discussion of movies and television shows. I casually lead a discussion about what television series or movies the students like or dislike. There will always be different points of view about this topic.

Select three or four movie trailers to show your students. Select trailers that students will have diverse opinions about. I often select a popular film with girls like the *Twilight* series, a superhero film, and a cartoon or kids' movie like *The Smurfs*. Most trailers are less than three minutes long and can be found online by searching for the movie title and the word trailer. IMDb.com is also a good resource with tons of movie trailers. Preview all trailers carefully for content and appropriateness.

1 Show students the first movie trailer. I try to make the first one the most relevant and engaging one that I can find.

2 After the trailer, ask students to give a thumbs up or thumbs down to indicate whether or not they would like to see that movie. Call on several students to explain why they would or would not go see the movie. Call on students until you have heard a variety of different viewpoints.

3 Repeat the thumbs up, thumbs down activity using a second movie trailer. You are building buy-in and interest here. This time, ask students to write three to five sentences to describe that movie. What would they write if they were trying to quickly tell another person what the film was about? Remind them that they can only base their description on what they saw or could infer from the movie trailer.

4 As students share verbally, listen for opposing perspectives. Select a few and record their descriptions on chart paper like the anchor chart here. Point out the differences in the adjectives and descriptions used to describe the same exact movie.

5 Repeat the activity with additional trailers as time allows. You will find that your students will love this and beg to do it multiple times. Honestly, I let them. What middle school student doesn't have an opinion or like to watch movie trailers? It is one of the happiest introductions that you can have for a skill.

6 When you wrap up the lesson, make sure that the chart paper descriptions are visible and point out that students have a lot of different ways to present information about a topic. *"This is also true when authors write about a subject. Two authors can both write about a past president, using many of the same facts, but have very different viewpoints. You can notice these differences by looking at how they describe things and what type of information they choose to share or not share."*

Final Destination Trailer

163

1 **Remind students of the activity they completed where the students talked about the same movies, but had different perspectives.** "*This happens a lot in writing as well. Sometimes it is very obvious and in your face. Other times it is much more subtle and you may not notice it as first. What I want to show you is how I think about text when I compare two different texts to determine how they present information differently.*"

2 **Using the opinions that the students voiced about the different movie trailers, create a large T-chart.** On this chart, write the statements or ideas that support the movie on one side and the statements or ideas that are against the movie on the other side. As you add ideas to each side, think out loud and wonder about each one. Point out how these ideas are all about one topic, but they show two different viewpoints.

3 **Now that you have created the T-chart from the movie trailers, you want to transition to a set of paired readings.** Select one set of paired readings to share with students. One example would be Francis and Manuel-Logan's pieces on Facebook. Each has a distinctly different viewpoint despite writing on the same topic. The suggested titles list includes multiple pairings to consider. When you select text, make sure that both pieces can be read independently by students as you read aloud. If you have the resources, project your text on the screen or even scan, make a transparency, or use your document camera so that you can model your reading. Create a T-chart to outline the differences between what the two authors say about your chosen topic.

164

The Smurfs Trailer

"This seems super cute. The little blue people of my childhood come alive! You have to admit—that's cool."

"Seriously? Is this a movie for people my age? The trailer is sending me to Sleepy Town."

"Cartoons and people in one movie? Been done. Epic fail."

"I caught myself laughing. The 'cool kids' might roll their eyes, but this movie has to cause a few laughs even among the super serious"

Standard 9: Different Viewpoints

Trailer: Smurfs Movie

-Adorable idea	-Too immature for most students
Creative	
-"Super Cute"	-Boring
-Connections to Childhood/ nostalgic	-Poor choice to combine real people+animation
-Great soundtrack	-Confusing story
-Funny jokes	-Tired + overdone concept

THE ORGANIZERS

Once you have explicitly introduced and modeled how to apply the strategies of the standard, now is the time to shift gears and provide students with multiple opportunities to practice the skill with their own reading in pairs, groups, and independently.

This standard requires careful text selection. You want to choose two or three pieces that explore the same topic, but have different ideas or arguments being made. This does not mean that you must have informational pieces that are opposites, but there should be areas of difference. I selected two free news articles that are available online (see the suggested list at the end of this chapter): *Bottled Water is Silly, But So is Banning It* and *Five Reasons Not to Drink Bottled Water*.

1 Read each article with your students. Model how to complete the organizer using the samples that I have modeled next to each organizer or complete your own sample from the blank copy found in each section.

2 Once you model by explicitly completing the organizer yourself, your students will see the connection between the informational text and the organizer. You can provide blank copies of the organizer and allow students to select their own informational text, assign one from your class anthology, or select a title from the suggested book list within this chapter.

3 Students can complete the organizer when they read *any* paired informational text sets. This can be done as an assignment and can be repeated as many times as you want with any informational sets that you choose. The sky is the limit! This allows for multiple opportunities to tailor the text to the student and maintain fidelity to the standard.

4 Once students have demonstrated mastery of the skill, don't stop using it. You want them to keep practicing. In the introduction of the book, I discussed the pitfalls of being a Checklist Teacher. Students need to keep perfecting their skill sets.

5 Reuse the same organizer, make it into an anchor chart, or post exemplars for students to reference later. You can add the organizer to a center or use it daily as evidence of reading.

165

FACE OFF!

Writing
Connection

This is also a great planner for a written piece comparing & contrasting two texts on similar topics.

Reinforce that students are looking for textual evidence to support where the texts agree or disagree.

Face Off!

Text #1
| Bottled Water is Silly, but so is banning it |

VS.

Text #2
| 5 Reasons Not to Drink Bottled Water |

Agree

- Bottled water is wasteful
- The bottled water industry is about $$
- Marketing makes bottled water seem better

Disagree

- Hypocritcal to ban water, but not soda
- Bottled water is a special indulgence
- Bans don't really make a difference

Students really get involved when I model this organizer. Agree vs. Disagree always sparks engagement!

A great extension here is to ask students to highlight the articles using two different colors to show areas of agreement or disagreement.

166

Face Off!

Text #1

VS.

Text #2

Agree

Disagree

©2013 The Common Core Guidebook. Intended for classroom use only. May not be reproduced or distributed without permission.

COMPARE VIEWPOINTS

I like to integrate informational text selections from science & social studies for this standard as well. This is a great way to use this skill across the curriculum.

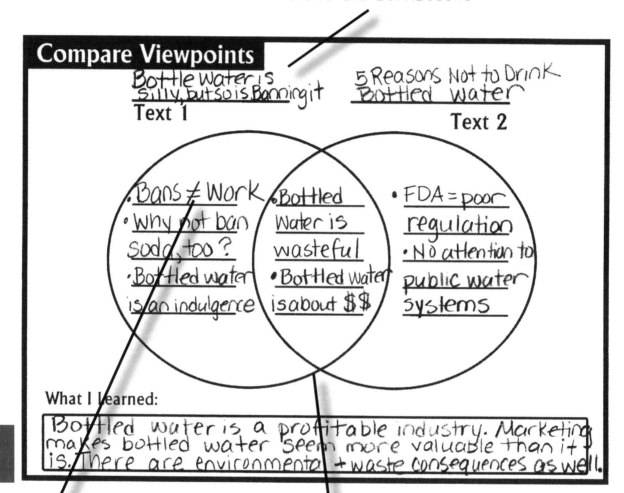

Compare Viewpoints

Bottle water is silly, but so is Banning it
Text 1

5 Reasons Not to Drink Bottled water
Text 2

- Bans ≠ Work
- Why not ban soda, too?
- Bottled water is an indulgence

- Bottled Water is wasteful
- Bottled Water is about $$

- FDA = poor regulation
- No attention to public water systems

What I learned:

Bottled water is a profitable industry. Marketing makes bottled water seem more valuable than it is. There are environmental + waste consequences as well.

whenever I model the organizers, I use & encourage students to use symbols like =, +, or other abbreviations. The focus is on ideas, not artificial length.

Venn diagrams offer students a familiar way to compare two different informational texts.

©2013 The Common Core Guidebook. Intended for classroom use only. May not be reproduced or distributed without permission.

Compare Viewpoints

Text 1

Text 2

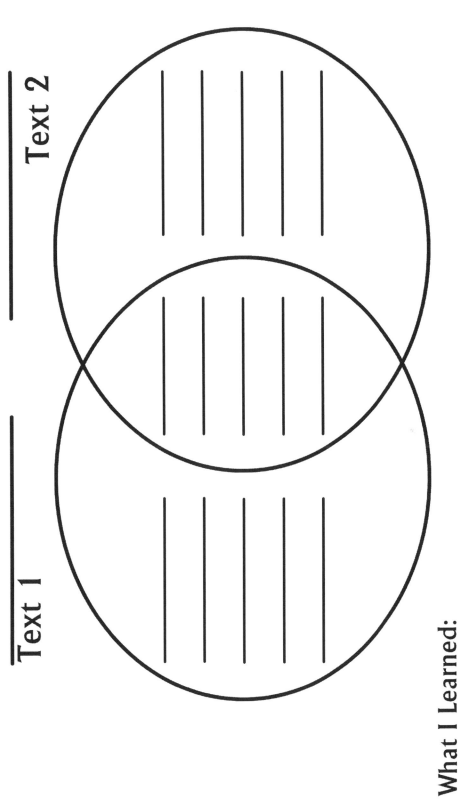

What I Learned:

THREE VIEWPOINTS

This organizer is a great choice for students to use when researching a topic to write about.

I like for students to choose a way to identify the text on their own. Author? Key word? Genre? Let them own it.

Writing Connection

Three Viewpoints

Topic: Value of Bottled Water?

	Event / Fact	Event / Fact	Event / Fact
Text 1 Fishman	Banning water is hypocritical —what about soda?	Bottled water is a profitable industry. $$	Bottled water creates a lot of waste.
Text 2 Wisconsin	Bottled water is not necessarily better than tap water.	FDA does regulate bottled water.	Lots of things can be done to make tap water taste better for less money. $
Text 3 Baskind	Bottled water is a $ money making industry.	FDA doesn't regulate water that stays within state lines.	Focus on bottled water causes many public water systems to be ignored.

When you model this organizer, you may want to break it up into more than one period or simply complete one text at a time.

©2013 The Common Core Guidebook. Intended for classroom use only. May not be reproduced or distributed without permission.

Three Viewpoints

Topic: _____

	Event / Fact	Event / Fact	Event / Fact
Text 1			
Text 2			
Text 3			

The suggested texts here are grouped based on the content or topic of the text. To meet the requirements of the standard, students need to be able to look at two or more different viewpoints about the same topic.

AMERICAN REVOLUTION

George vs. George: The American Revolution as Seen from Both Sides
Rosalyn Schanze
ISBN: 978-1709789907
This historical fiction text offers multiple perspectives in one place. Different viewpoints are used to tell about the events of the American Revolution. Nontraditional perspectives really make this text stand out from more traditional texts.

ARTIFICIAL SWEETENERS

Artificial Sweeteners: Sugar-free, but at What Cost?
Holly Strawbridge
http://www.health.harvard.edu/blog/artificial-sweeteners-sugar-free-but-at-what-cost-201207165030
This informational text article examines the effects of a sugar-free diet supplemented with artificial sweeteners. Relying on data from the American Heart Association and the American Diabetes Association, this article is rich with quotes and hyperlinks to additional data.

Dr. Keri Peterson on Dr. Oz "Artificial Sweeteners"
YouTube
https://www.youtube.com/watch?v=A-hUyw2lcio
This YouTube video discusses the impact of sugar substitutes. Presenting myth and fact, the six-minute segment provides a quick and easy to understand set of facts about aspartame, saccharin, and sucralose. Dr. Oz presents a series of questions and concerns about sugar alternatives to Dr. Keri Peterson. She argues that artificial sweeteners are safe. Be careful to review the associated videos or ads that may be included on the sidebars. There may be inappropriate links to videos or advertisements.

Bottled Water Usage

Five Reasons Not to Drink Bottled Water
Chris Baskind
http://www.mnn.com/food/healthy-eating/stories/5-reasons-not-to-drink-bottled-water
The article makes the argument that bottled water is no better than tap water. The author presents five key reasons why consumers should opt for water from the tap over bottled choices. Exploring the role that marketing has on consumer decisions to purchase bottled water, the text is an excellent example of crafting an argument and supporting it with details.

Bottled Water is Silly — But So is Banning It
Charles Fishman
http://newswatch.nationalgeographic.com/2012/02/13/bottled-water-is-silly-but-so-is-banning-it/
This *National Geographic* article discusses bottled water use. The author presents a nuanced argument and is a bit tongue-in-cheek. The author's tone and his word choices are worth discussing. Students get to see an example of an informational text that also has a clear voice.

Tap Water, Bottled Water, Filtered Water: Which to Choose?
http://www.foodsafety.wisc.edu/consumer/fact_sheets/waterbottles.pdf
This article uses bullets, labeled images, and hyperlinks to present the pros and cons of each type of water. Presented in a simple, three-page format, this article is a straightforward example of an argument with support. The article explains factors that may influence the safety of tap water, along with the procedure for processing bottled water. This short article is a great piece to read with students and discuss the central ideas of the text and supporting evidence.

Censorship, Recycling, Green Energy, Child Soldiers

Columbia Teachers College: Reading and Writing Project
http://readingandwritingproject.com/public/themes/rwproject/resources/booklists/nonfiction%20sets/Middle_School_Nonfiction_Text_Sets.pdf
This document has links to sets of informational text (about five per topic) that present opposing viewpoints on different subjects ranging from the Occupy Wall Street Movement to school lunch. These sources provide ready-to-use articles for this standard. Originally designed to help students with argument writing, these articles offer numerous other applications for instruction.

FACEBOOK

Is Facebook Bad for Kids?
Enjoli Francis
http://abcnews.go.com/Technology/Family/facebook-bad-kids-psychologist-talks-social-medias-pros/story?id=14271651
This short *ABC News* article (about half a page) presents expert quotations, hyperlinks, images, and a video excerpt to answer the question: *Should kids use Facebook?* This text can be used as a catalyst to discuss different ways that authors present evidence.

Study: Facebook Teaches Kids Freedom of Speech
Ruth Manuel-Logan
http://allfacebook.com/study-facebook-teaches-kids-freedom-of-speech_b58683
This article is a brief news piece that supports the use of Facebook for students. The article presents a wide range of evidence that Facebook provides an appreciation of free speech in a way that school does not.

FRACKING

The Facts on Fracking
The New York Times
http://www.nytimes.com/2013/03/14/opinion/global/the-facts-on-fracking.html
This article is developed as a clear argument with varying evidence. The structure offers students multiple areas to consider and evaluate. Fracking is a topic that few will be familiar with, so it also offers a content area that students can consider without prior bias or a predetermined side. This creates a great opportunity to simply consider the evidence presented.

The Real Story Behind the Fracking Debate
Peter Gleick
http://www.huffingtonpost.com/peter-h-gleick/the-real-story-behind-the_1_b_1719554.html
This article begins with the idea that fracking is neither good nor bad. The article presents a series of facts that explain what fracking is, why it is used, and the potential risks and benefits. This is excellent for evaluating evidence and claims.

What is Fracking?
Shale Energy
http://www.energyfromshale.org/hydraulic-fracturing/what-is-fracking?
This article presents an argument for fracking. Students are presented with reasons why this practice is a critical component of America's future energy plan. Using images and text, the article presents information and details to support the expansion and use of fracking as a national effort.

Global Warming

An Inconvenient Truth

Al Gore

Paramount: 2006

This well-known documentary chronicles the consequences of global warming. Footage and interviews are used to make the case for increased awareness and action to help halt global warming. This documentary offers readers an excellent opportunity to examine word choice and evidence.

The Sky's Not Falling! Why It's OK to Chill About Global Warming

Holly Fretwell

ISBN: 978-0976726944

Fretwell's controversial text is a counterargument to the claim that global warming is a critical problem. The author presents an argument that global warming is really not an important concern. Encouraging readers to "just chill," Fretwell insists that the media is simply indoctrinating teens with a false sense of urgency and fear about the climate.

New York Times Global Warming Archive

http://topics.nytimes.com/top/news/science/topics/globalwarming/index.html

This is the *New York Times* archive of global warming articles. This source provides a wealth of different articles on global warming. It lists them in reverse chronological order, providing easy access to the most recent. I find that these articles present a clear point of view and offer excellent examples of claims, evidence, and varying word choices.

Homework

As Homework Grows, So do Arguments Against It

Valerie Strauss

Washington Post

http://www.washingtonpost.com/wp-dyn/content/article/2006/09/11/AR2006091100908_pf.html

This article features myriad facts from experts and professors coupled with interviews with kids. Organized to present clear evidence and facts, the article outlines the arguments against homework in a lucid manner. This is an excellent choice for examining evidence and different viewpoints.

Duke Study: Homework Helps Students Succeed in School, As Long as There Isn't Too Much

Kelly Gilmer

http://today.duke.edu/2006/03/homework.html

This very brief article argues that homework does have value. The author outlines the evidence that supports this claim. Students can examine the author's viewpoint and its development.

Homework: New Research Suggests it May Be an Unnecessary Evil
Alfie Kohn
http://www.huffingtonpost.com/alfie-kohn/homework-research_b_2184918.html
This article presents research that suggests that homework offers a limited benefit. The organization and support for claims are just two of the benefits of using this text. Students can also consider crafting their own written pieces based on research from this article. Always a claim that students tend to agree with, this argument promotes engagement and discussion.

Today's Assignment
Louis Menand
The New Yorker
http://www.newyorker.com/talk/comment/2012/12/17/121217taco_talk_menand
This article begins by explaining that the president of France has the ability to abolish homework for all students. The article then continues to make a case against homework. Note: I would copy and paste the text of this article into a Microsoft Word™ document and display it or make photocopies. When I first read this article, it was coupled with racy pictures from another *New Yorker* article.

The Great Homework Debate:
Is Homework Helpful or Harmful to Students?
Cory Ames
http://www.scilearn.com/blog/homework-debate-is-homework-helpful-or-harmful.php
This article looks at homework from a neutral position. The author evaluates the purpose and structure of homework assignments in school. Hyperlinks and references to sources are included, making this is an excellent informational text to examine for evidence.

TITANIC

Gilded Lives, Fatal Voyage:
The Titanic's First-Class Passengers and Their World
Hugh Brewster
ISBN: 978-0307984708
This text chronicles the lives of the first-class passengers onboard the Titanic. While this is a rich informational text, the most effective part of the book is the final chapter, *The Post Script: Titanic Afterlives*. This chapter provides a narrative account of the survivors' lives after the Titanic.

Shadow of the Titanic: The Extraordinary Stories of Those Who Survived
Andrew Wilson
ISBN: 978-1451671568
This text is based on the diaries, memories, letters, and interviews of the surviving members of the Titanic. Students can read specific chapters that follow individual survivors. The chapters chronicle how they remember that fateful day and how they coped after the event. Filled with colorful language, this text can be used in multiple ways to model the informational text standards.

Akhondi, M., Aziz Malayeri, F., & Samad, A. A. (2011). How to teach expository text structure to facilitate reading comprehension. *The Reading Teacher, 64*(5), 368–372.

Almasi, J. F., & Fullerton, S. K. (2012). *Teaching strategic processes in reading.* New York: Guilford.

Anderson, R. C. (1984). Role of reader's schema in comprehension, learning and memory. In R. Anderson, J. Osborne, and R. Tierney (Eds.), *Learning to read in American schools.* Hillsdale, NJ: Lawrence Erlbaum Associates.

Anderson, R. C. (1995). *Research foundations for wide reading.* Urbana, IL: Center for the Study of Reading, Special Invitational Conference.

Baumann, J. F., Jones, L. A., & Seifert-Kessell, N. (1993). Using think-alouds to enhance children's comprehension monitoring abilities. *The Reading Teacher, 47*(3), 184-193.

Beers, K. (2003). *When kids can't read: What teachers can do.* Portsmouth, NH: Heinemann.

Caldwell, K., & Gaine, T. (2000). 'The Phantom Tollbooth' and how the independent reading of good books improves students' reading performance. San Rafael, CA: Reading and Communication Skills Clearinghouse. (ERIC Document Reproduction Service No. ED449462).

Duke, N. K., Pearson, P. D., Strachan, S. L., & Billman, A. K. (2011). Essential elements of fostering and teaching reading comprehension. In S. Samuels and A. Farstrup, *What research has to say about reading instruction* (pp. 94-114). Newark, DE: International Reading Association.

Fisher, D.. & Frey, N. (2007). *Checking for understanding: Formative assessment techniques for your classroom.* Alexandria, VA: Association for Supervision & Curriculum Development (ASCD).

Frey, N., & Fisher, D. (2010). Identifying instructional moves during guided learning. *The Reading Teacher, 64*(2), 84–95.

Frayer, D., Frederick, W. C., & Klausmeier, H. J. (1969). *A schema for testing the level of cognitive mastery.* Madison, WI: Wisconsin Center for Education Research.

Gallagher, K. (2004). *Deeper reading: Comprehending challenging texts.* Portland, ME: Stenhouse.

Gee, J. (2004). *Situated language and learning: A critique of traditional schooling.* New York: Routledge.

Harvey, S., & Goudvis, A. (2000). *Strategies that work: Teaching comprehension to enhance understanding.* Portland, ME: Stenhouse.

Hinchman, K. A., & Sheridan-Thomas, H. (2008). *Best practices in adolescent literacy instruction (solving problems in the teaching of literacy).* New York: The Guilford Press.

179

Mandel Morrow, L., & Gambrell, L. B. (2011). *Best practices in literacy instruction* (4th ed.). New York: The Guilford Press.

National Governors Association Center for Best Practices and Council of Chief State School Officers. (2010). *Common Core state standards.* Retrieved May 4, 2012 from http://www.corestandards.org.

National Institute of Child Health and Human Development. (2000). *Report of the National Reading Panel: Teaching children to read, an evidence-based assessment of the scientific research literature on reading and its implications for reading instruction.* Washington, DC: U.S. Government Printing Office.

Oster, L. (2001). Using the think-aloud for reading instruction. *The Reading Teacher, 55*(1), 64-69.

Polikoff, M. S. (2012). Instructional alignment under No Child Left Behind. *American Journal of Education, 118(3)*, 341-368.

Spillane, J. P. (2004). *Standards deviation: How schools misunderstand education policy.* Cambridge, MA: Harvard University Press.

Tierney, R., & Shanahan, T. (1996). Research on the reading writing relationship. In R. Barr, M. Kamil, P. Mosenthal, & P. D. Pearson (Eds.), *Handbook of reading research 2* (pp. 246–274). Mahwah, NJ: Lawrence Erlbaum.

Todaro, S. A., Millis, K. K., & Dandotkar, S. (2010). The impact of semantic and causal relatedness and reading skill on standards of coherence. *Discourse Processes, 47*, 421-446.

Wiggins, G. (2005). *Understanding by design.* Alexandria, VA: Association for Supervision & Curriculum Development (ASCD).

Vygotsky, L. S. (1978). *Mind in society: The development of higher psychological processes.* Cambridge, MA: Harvard University Press.

Zwiers, J. (2005). *Building reading comprehension habits in grades 6–12.* Newark, DE: International Reading Association.

ABOUT THE AUTHOR

Rozlyn Linder, Ph.D., is a highly sought-after presenter. Known for her energetic, fast-paced seminars and workshops, she has traveled throughout the United States to collaborate with teachers at national and state conferences on literacy. An award-winning teacher, she has taught at all levels from elementary through college. She is passionate about motivating students through explicit instruction and the development of standards-based classrooms. Rozlyn and her husband, Chris, have two spirited daughters.